Handfuls *of* Sunshine

*For Mum and Dad, thank you for
teaching me about food and love.
And for Olive, Kip and Slav, always.*

Handfuls *of* Sunshine

TILLY PAMMENT

murdoch books

Sydney | London

Contents

Baby Cakes & Buttery Bliss ___ 113

Baby Cakes

Apricot, Polenta & Saffron Tea Cakes

Blackberry, Bay & White Chocolate Muffins

Sticky Prune, Pear & Ginger Cakes with Ginger Caramel

Little Pound Cakes

Quince & Frangipane Cakes (GF)

Cardamom, Bay & Orange Madeleines

Coconut & Passionfruit Loaves

Mango & Passionfruit Cream Cakes

Strawberry & Rhubarb Jam Victoria Sponges

Blueberry, Coconut & Lemon Bars (GF)

Sunken Chocolate Cheesecakes (GF)

Hazelnut Lamington Fingers

Sugared Scones, Pikelets & Sticky Buns ___ 151

Buttermilk Pikelets

Coconut Buns

Date & Ginger Scones

Sugared Buttermilk & Lemon Scones

Cardamom Tea Buns

Pumpkin & Prune Scones

Apple & Cinnamon Streuselkuchen

Apricot & Sultana Hot Cross Buns

Pantry Keepers & Postable Love ___ 179

Lemon & Fennel Seed Amaretti (GF)

Apricot Shortbread Slice

Double Chocolate & Ginger Biscotti

Earl Grey & Polenta Rounds

Sour Cherry, Pistachio & Rose Rocky Road (GF)

Chai & Almond Crescents

Malted Hazelnut Blondies

Cinnamon Maple Stars (GF)

Gently Spiced Gingerbread

Puddles of Jam & Sweet Baked Fruit ___ 205

Roast Apricot Jam

Plum & Star Anise Jam

Passionfruit Curd

Strawberry & Rhubarb Jam

Baked Stone Fruit

Marmalade Baked Rhubarb

Baked Quince

Good Fruit Mince

Introduction

Food is the language in which I am most fluent: a primary means of communication and connection in my life and in the lives of those with whom I surround myself.

If everyday cooking is essential communication, then sweet baking is my love language. It is what I turn to for little pockets of joy; handfuls of sunshine, sticky with jam and vanilla; kind words and warm embraces in the form of sugar, butter and biscuit crumbs. It is messy and imperfect, but full of love. Of generosity, joy and connection. Of burnt butter, chocolate, spice and sprinkles. Passionfruit curd and coconut. Sticky, sweet and sunshiny delicious.

For me, sweet baking is life-enhancing. It is a joy-creator and a bringer of light when things feel dark.

In this book you will find a collection of small, unfussy sweet bakes, including slices, biscuits, tarts, cakes, scones, buns and other bite-sized beauties.

They are things designed to be held in our hands, shared with others, or squirrelled away for a rainy day.

They are the petite sweet treats that frequent my family's table; the recipes that are baked and eaten still warm from the oven when they're really too hot to hold, nibbled at with hungry fingers and sugary lips.

They are the little bakes that are made and gifted to friends and family in need of a little solace, or just a sugar-crusted 'hello'!

They are the things that bring a little extra sunshine, comfort, connection and joy to our days, weeks and years. The bakes that cocoon us when we are down, the ones we share with greedy glee at celebrations, the ones wrapped with care and sent off in the mail to loved ones far away, and the ones I tuck away, secretly, to enjoy another day.

They are the recipes that I love to cook and eat (sometimes in lieu of dinner!), and my hope is that you will love them too.

This book is filled with sunshine to share! It is my take on simple, sweet, home baking; childhood favourites and nostalgic treats; and the little luxuries that make life all the sweeter. Life is complicated enough already, baking doesn't have to be.

Useful kitchen notes

Tablespoon measurements An Australian tablespoon measure, which is 20 ml (¾ fl oz/ 4 teaspoons), has been used to test all the recipes in this book. If you are using a 15 ml (½ fl oz/3 teaspoon) tablespoon, simply add an additional 1 teaspoon of ingredient for every 1 tablespoon listed.

Oven temperatures All the recipes in this book have been tested in domestic ovens using the fan-forced setting. If using a conventional oven setting, increase the temperature by 20°C (35°F). It is also worth noting that all ovens cook differently, and therefore cooking times may need to be adjusted slightly depending on your oven. Use your intuition, nose and baking experience with your own oven as a guide here! An oven thermometer is also useful to check that your oven is cooking at the temperature at which it is set.

Eggs The recipes use 59 g (2¼ oz) – including shell – free-range eggs. These are sold as 'extra-large' eggs in Australia (700 g/1 lb 9 oz minimum weight per dozen). I always buy free-range eggs, and organic when possible. It is always best to use room-temperature eggs when baking, as they combine more easily with other ingredients. This allows more air to be trapped in batters and doughs, making for lighter cakes and biscuits. If you have forgotten to take your eggs out of the fridge before you want to bake, place them in a bowl of warm water for 5 minutes or so before using.

Lining a cake or slice (slab) tin Greasing and lining tins is one of the most tedious, yet essential, skills when baking. Skip or rush this step and you may pay for it with a bake that sticks, or doesn't turn out as beautifully as you'd hoped. I have found the best method for lining cake tins is to use a pastry brush to coat the tin well with very soft butter. Then either dust with a few teaspoons of plain (all-purpose) flour, tapping out any excess, or line the base and sides with baking paper.

When lining a slice tin, use a single sheet of baking paper larger than your tin and line it in one piece, folding and pleating the paper in place at the corners. I then use small metal bulldog (letter) clips to hold the paper in place while the slice bakes. The extra baking paper can then be used to help lift the whole slice out of the tin when cooked and cooled for ease of slicing.

Checking whether a bake is cooked I use a thin metal cake tester to check whether my bakes are cooked, but a wooden or metal skewer works well too. Simply insert the tester in the centre of your bake, count to five, then remove it gently. If the tester comes out clean, the cake is cooked. If it has wet batter or lots of moist crumbs clinging to it, your bake needs a bit longer in the oven (the exceptions here are things like brownies, blondies and cheesecakes, which still need to be a little wobbly when removed from the oven). Also look at the sides of the bake right next to the tin – when cooked they tend to shrink away slightly from the edge of the tin. Take extra care when baking little cakes, as it doesn't take much to overcook such small items.

Sterilising jars for jam or curd To sterilise jars, wash glass jars and metal lids in hot soapy water and rinse well, or wash jars and lids in a dishwasher. Put the clean jars upright on a baking tray lined with baking paper and place in a preheated oven at 120°C (250°F) fan-forced for about 10 minutes or until thoroughly dry. Meanwhile, put metal lids in a small saucepan and cover with boiling water. Boil for 10 minutes, remove from the saucepan and dry well with clean paper towel. Remove the jars from the oven, fill with hot jam and seal while hot. Unopened jam will store well in a cool place for a couple of months. Once opened, store in the refrigerator and use within a month. Store curd in a sealed jar in the fridge and consume within a week.

Roasting nuts Place the nuts on a baking tray in a low oven (120°C/250°F fan-forced) until toasty all the way through, about 5–10 minutes. To remove skins from hazelnuts, place the roasted nuts in a clean tea towel (dish towel) and rub together to remove most of the skins. Allow the nuts to cool before blitzing or using as directed in recipes.

POSTING BAKED GOODS

Many of the biscuits and slices in this book (especially the ones from the Pantry Keepers & Postable Love chapter) can easily be packed and posted in the mail to loved ones all over the country. I do this often – and love the thought of an unsuspecting friend or family member opening the door to a little box of sunshine left sitting on their doorstep!

Shelf life Make sure your bakes are as fresh as can be (but completely cool) when you post them. Have a look at how long they'll keep, and make sure to take into consideration how long it will take for them to arrive by mail. Express post is the best option to ensure your bakes arrive in plenty of time for the recipient to enjoy them.

It's a good idea to include a note that mentions a 'best-before' date, and a list of ingredients for the bakes too.

Packaging Make sure to wrap and seal your bakes well in at least one airtight layer of food-safe cellophane or a plastic snaplock bag. I then wrap my bakes in a layer of tissue or brown paper (or foil for chocolatey bakes). A layer of honeycomb paper or bubble wrap is a good idea too when sending biscuits. Place your wrapped bakes snugly in a postage box (always a box, not a postage bag!), and pad with extra paper or bubble wrap to make sure the bakes can't move around in transit. If there is movement, there is a danger that things will get squashed or broken. If packing multiple bakes, pack sturdier things on the bottom, followed by biscuits or more delicate things on top.

Weather Take into consideration the weather before you post your bakes. If it is very hot, it's best not to post any bakes with chocolate in them. Melty puddles of chocolate, while delicious, are not what we're going for here!

Little extras As the song goes, 'brown paper packages tied up with strings, these are a few of my favourite things', and so they are! Include pretty washi tape and cute cardboard swing tags and I think you've really hit the sweet spot! If you have the time and inclination, a little extra care when wrapping your baked goods – coloured tape and ribbon, or candles for a birthday box – can make all the difference. I have a little box full of ribbons and string I've saved from birthdays, and I regularly raid this for a little extra cheer when wrapping parcels.

Bars of sunny lemon and passionfruit, mango and lime. Squares of rich chocolate and marmalade, nuts and caramel. Pillows of blossom-scented meringue and apricot jam. These are the slices that speckle my days and weeks, bringing handfuls of sunshine and joy to share.

There is an innate generosity to be found in a homemade slice – an uncomplicated joy that is the traybake. It is the memories of childhood, sliced up and ready to be shared; snatched up by hungry hands and sugary lips, coming back again and again, for simple, sweet delight.

Homemade Sunbeams & Slices of Joy

Australian summer in a slice tin. These flavours will forever remind me of camping holidays at the beach as a kid; when life was simple and the only real dilemma was whether to have a mango Weis Bar™ or a Frosty Fruit™. A Weis Bar usually won out. Then, when we'd return from the beach salty, sandy, a little bit cranky and in need of food and a rest, there was usually a tray of mangoes sitting on the tailgate of the camper trailer. Dad would peel them for us using his super sharp filleting knife and order would be restored, at least for a while. Fruit therapy at its finest. Rather like this slice!

Mango & Lime Cheesecake Bars

MAKES ONE 20 X 30 CM (8 X 12 INCH) SLICE (15 PIECES)

BASE

125 g (4½ oz) plain (all-purpose) flour

100 g (3½ oz) desiccated coconut

80 g (2¾ oz) caster (superfine) sugar

⅛ teaspoon fine sea salt

125 g (4½ oz) unsalted butter, melted and cooled

TOPPING

250 g (9 oz) cream cheese

Finely grated zest and juice of 1 lime

200 g (7 oz) sour cream

110 g (3¾ oz) caster (superfine) sugar

2 teaspoons vanilla bean paste

2 eggs, lightly beaten

1 tablespoon plain (all-purpose) flour

1 large ripe mango

Line the base and sides of a 20 x 30 cm (8 x 12 inch) slice (slab) or lamington tin with baking paper, leaving enough paper overhanging to help lift the cooked slice out of the tin. Take the cream cheese and sour cream (for the topping) out of the fridge to come to room temperature while you make the base.

Make the base by combining the flour, desiccated coconut, sugar and salt in a mixing bowl. Make a well in the centre and pour in the melted butter. Mix with a wooden spoon until well combined. Tip the rubbly mixture into the base of your prepared tin and press out firmly into an even layer. Place the tin in the fridge (or freezer if you have space), until well chilled and firm.

While the base is chilling, preheat the oven to 170°C (325°F) fan-forced.

When firm, bake in the preheated oven for 15–20 minutes or until golden and smelling deliciously toasty. Allow to cool slightly while you make the cheesecake topping.

Lower the oven temperature to 140°C (275°F). Place the cream cheese and lime zest in the bowl of a stand mixer with a paddle attachment and mix on low speed until smooth. Add the sour cream, sugar, vanilla and eggs and mix again, scraping down the side of the bowl a few times until the mixture is smooth. Lastly, sift in the flour and mix briefly to combine. Set aside. →

Peel and roughly chop the mango and place it, along with the lime juice, in a small blender or food processor and blitz until smooth. Fold half of this through the cream cheese mixture before pouring the cream cheese mixture on top of the cooked base. Smooth the surface and dot the top with spoonfuls of the remaining mango and lime puree. Run a knife gently through the surface of the slice to create a decorative effect – I do this in lines through the mango puree to create little heart patterns, because I'm a hopeless romantic, but you do whatever works for you! Bake in the preheated oven for 30–35 minutes. The surface of the slice should be set, but there should still be a slight wobble in the middle when you jiggle the tin.

Allow the slice to cool completely in the tin before placing it in the fridge to chill for a couple of hours (or overnight). To serve, slice into bars with a hot, sharp knife.

STORE & SHARE *This slice is best eaten cold, within 2–3 days of baking. Keep any leftovers in an airtight container in the fridge, sneaking a piece when you think no one is looking! (Or run a plate over to your neighbours and enjoy being their favourite … at least momentarily.)*

Inspired by the British classic, Bakewell tart, this simple slice is comforting in the extreme. A layer of almond biscuit base and frangipane sandwich a tart plum jam filling, which is the perfect foil for the buttery almond exterior. Slice it into fingers and serve it for morning or afternoon tea (although I have been known to eat it for breakfast, and can recommend it with a nice strong cup of tea!). I am going to be bossy here, though, and insist that you make this slice with really good jam – if not my Plum & Star Anise Jam (page 207), then another deliciously tart fruity number please!

Bakewell Slice

MAKES ONE 20 X 30 CM (8 X 12 INCH) SLICE (15 PIECES)

320 g (11¼ oz) Plum & Star Anise
 Jam (page 207), or tart jam of
 your choice
50 g (1¾ oz) flaked almonds
Icing (confectioners') sugar, to
 dust

BASE
150 g (5½ oz) white spelt flour
75 g (2½ oz) almond meal
80 g (2¾ oz) caster (superfine)
 sugar
⅛ teaspoon fine sea salt
125 g (4½ oz) unsalted butter,
 melted and cooled

FRANGIPANE
125 g (4½ oz) unsalted butter,
 softened
110 g (3¾ oz) caster (superfine)
 sugar
1 teaspoon vanilla bean paste

Ingredients continued over page

Line the base and sides of a 20 x 30 cm (8 x 12 inch) slice (slab) or lamington tin with baking paper, leaving enough paper overhanging to help lift the cooked slice out of the tin.

First, make the base by combining the spelt flour, almond meal, sugar and salt in a mixing bowl. Make a well in the centre and pour in the melted butter. Mix with a wooden spoon or spatula until combined. Tip the mixture into the base of your prepared tin and press out into an even layer using an offset palette knife or the bottom of a glass. Place the tin in the fridge (or freezer if you have space), until well chilled and firm.

While the base is chilling, preheat the oven to 170°C (325°F) fan-forced.

When chilled, prick the base all over with a fork and bake in the preheated oven for 15–20 minutes or until golden brown and smelling deliciously toasty. Allow to cool slightly while you make the frangipane.

Lower the oven temperature to 160°C (325°F). In the bowl of a stand mixer with a paddle attachment, cream the butter, sugar, vanilla and almond extract (if using), until light and fluffy. Add the eggs, one at a time, beating well after each addition. Stir in the almond meal, followed by the spelt flour, baking powder and salt, then beat for a minute or so on medium speed until the mixture is light. →

**BAKEWELL SLICE
CONTINUED**

¼ teaspoon almond extract
  (optional, but delicious)
2 eggs
150 g (5½ oz) almond meal
2 tablespoons white spelt flour
½ teaspoon baking powder
Pinch of fine sea salt

Spread the plum and star anise jam in an even layer over the cooked slice base (removing any star anise pieces). Top with the frangipane and use a spatula to smooth it out as evenly as you can. The jam will probably squidge up a bit through the frangipane in some places, but that's okay – we're aiming for delicious, not perfect! Scatter the flaked almonds over the top, then bake in the preheated oven for 30–40 minutes, or until the frangipane is golden and cooked through.

Allow the slice to cool completely in the tin before lifting it out. Slice into bars with a sharp knife and dust with icing sugar just before serving.

STORE & SHARE *Best served on the day it is baked, with a big pot of tea in the sunshine with dear friends (or a good book)! Any leftovers will keep well in an airtight container in a cool place for 2–3 days.*

Any bake with passionfruit in it sings 'sunshine' to me and, when combined with the sharp, fresh flavour of lemon, I feel you really can't go wrong. This sunny-yellow, curd-topped slice is for days when a little BYO sunshine is required – for the ones that are a tad lacklustre, or just require a bit of extra oomph. I like to think of it as therapy in colour and culinary form. Sweet, mouth-puckering joy. Slice it, eat it, and share the sunshine around!

Passionfruit Sunshine Slice

MAKES ONE 20 X 30 CM (8 X 12 INCH) SLICE (18 PIECES)

BASE

225 g (8 oz) plain (all-purpose) flour

60 g (2¼ oz) desiccated coconut

110 g (3¾ oz) caster (superfine) sugar

¼ teaspoon fine sea salt

150 g (5½ oz) unsalted butter, melted and cooled

1 teaspoon vanilla bean paste

PASSIONFRUIT TOPPING

220 g (7¾ oz) caster (superfine) sugar

50 g (1¾ oz) plain (all-purpose) flour

Pinch of fine sea salt

6 eggs

150 g (5 oz) sour cream, stirred until smooth

Line the base and sides of a 20 x 30 cm (8 x 12 inch) slice (slab) or lamington tin with baking paper, leaving enough paper overhanging to help lift the cooked slice out of the tin.

First, make the base by combining the flour, coconut, sugar and salt in a mixing bowl. Make a well in the centre of the dry ingredients, pour in the melted butter and vanilla, and use a wooden spoon to mix to a crumbly dough. Tip the mixture into the base of your prepared tin and press it out into an even layer using an offset palette knife or the bottom of a glass. Make sure to press the mixture right into the corners and sides of the tin so that the topping doesn't leak out around the sides when added later. Place the tin in the fridge (or freezer if you have space), until well chilled and firm.

While the base is chilling, preheat the oven to 170°C (325°F) fan-forced.

When chilled, bake in the preheated oven for 20–25 minutes or until golden brown and smelling deliciously toasty.

While the base is cooking, make the passionfruit topping by mixing the sugar, flour and salt together in a mixing bowl. Add the eggs and whisk until combined, but not aerated. Whisk in the sour cream, followed by the lemon zest and juice, and half the passionfruit pulp. Set aside and let the mixture stand while the base cooks. →

Ingredients continued over page

Finely grated zest of 1 lemon

125 ml (4 fl oz) lemon juice (from
   3–4 lemons)

125 ml (4 fl oz) fresh passionfruit
   pulp (from 5–6 passionfruit)

When the base is cooked, lower the oven temperature to 140°C (275°F), leaving the tin in the oven. Use a fine sieve to strain the topping into another bowl, discarding the seeds and any lumps. Skim off any foam from the surface, add the remaining passionfruit pulp and stir it through. Carefully pour the passionfruit mixture on top of the cooked base – I do this while the tin is in the oven as I find it easier than juggling the whole thing back into the oven with the runny topping!

Bake the slice for a further 16–22 minutes, or until the surface of the topping is just set, but is still a little wobbly in the centre when you gently jiggle the tin. The curd will continue to cook as it cools and if you overcook the topping it may crack while cooling. This won't affect the flavour at all; it just makes it look a little less pretty. Allow the slice to cool to room temperature before placing the tin in the fridge for a couple of hours, until well chilled.

When ready to serve, use the extra baking paper to lift the slice from the tin. Use a large sharp knife to cut the slice into bars, wiping the knife clean between cuts. Serve cold or at room temperature with a large pot of tea.

 STORE & SHARE *Store any leftovers in an airtight container in the fridge for up to 2 days.*

A crackly chocolate crust; soft, fudgy middle; and short, buttery, biscuit base. What's not to love? I like to think of this as a slice that has grown up and seen the world – less of a pretty face and more of a layered, complex individual. Have I lost you yet ...? Yes, we are talking about a slice! Let's just say it's good. The marmalade is just a whisper among the dark chocolate here, not a citrussy shout, which is just how I like it.

Chocolate & Marmalade Shortbread Squares

MAKES ONE 20 CM (8 INCH) SQUARE SLICE (12 PIECES)

SHORTBREAD BASE
125 g (4½ oz) unsalted butter, softened
55 g (2 oz) caster (superfine) sugar
1 teaspoon vanilla bean paste
100 g (3½ oz) plain (all-purpose) flour
50 g (1¾ oz) white rice flour
⅛ teaspoon fine sea salt
¼ teaspoon baking powder

TOPPING
120 g (4¼ oz) dark chocolate (45–55% cocoa solids), roughly chopped
80 g (2¾ oz) unsalted butter
80 g (2¾ oz) caster (superfine) sugar
2 eggs
Pinch of fine sea salt
1 teaspoon vanilla bean paste

Ingredients continued over page

Line the base and sides of a 20 cm (8 inch) square cake tin with baking paper, leaving enough paper overhanging to help lift the cooked slice out of the tin.

First, make the base by placing the butter, sugar and vanilla in the bowl of a stand mixer with a paddle attachment. Beat until light and fluffy before adding the plain flour, rice flour, salt and baking powder to the bowl, stirring gently until the dough just comes together. Tip the mixture into the base of your prepared tin and use your hands, or an offset palette knife, to gently press it out into an even layer. Place the tin in the fridge (or freezer if you have space), until well chilled and firm.

While the base is chilling, preheat the oven to 140°C (275°F) fan-forced.

When firm, prick the base all over with a fork and bake in the preheated oven for 30–35 minutes or until the shortbread is just starting to colour and the surface is set. Remove from the oven and allow to cool slightly. Increase the oven temperature to 160°C (325°F).

While the base is baking, start the chocolate topping by combining the chocolate and butter in a small saucepan. Heat over very low heat, stirring often, until the chocolate and butter have melted into a glorious, smooth chocolate puddle. Set aside to cool slightly. →

**CHOCOLATE & MARMALADE
SHORTBREAD SQUARES
CONTINUED**

**1 tablespoon plain (all-purpose)
flour**
**2 tablespoons orange
marmalade**

When the base is cooked, place the sugar, eggs and salt in the bowl of a stand mixer with a whisk attachment and whisk on medium-high speed until the mixture is pale, very light and fluffy, 3–5 minutes. Fold through the melted chocolate mixture, along with the vanilla. Once incorporated, sift in the plain flour and gently fold it through.

Spread the marmalade evenly over the cooked base, then pour the chocolate topping over. Place the slice back in the oven to bake for 15–20 minutes, or until the surface is set, but the topping is still a little wobbly underneath. Allow to cool completely in the tin, before slicing and serving. Eat one piece standing over the chopping board as you cut the slice – quality control and all that! (You can refrigerate the slice for a couple of hours before slicing if you like – this makes it easier to get neat slices, but as I like the slice soft and mousse-y, I accept my slices slightly squiffy!)

STORE & SHARE *This slice is also a tried-and-tested teacher bribe! Bundle up a few slices and take to school at pick-up time, thereby ensuring your child is the class favourite, at least for a few days! Store any leftovers in an airtight container in the fridge for up to 3 days, returning to room temperature before serving.*

In my experience, good muesli bars are few and far between. Never having warmed to the commercially produced variety, I'm slightly embarrassed to say that it has taken me until well into my thirties to realise that homemade (of course) is the way to go! Then you can put only the best bits in – oats, tart dried apricots, coconut and almonds are my personal favourites, but feel free to experiment here, and leave out any bits you don't like!

These are exceptionally easy to make ... and the resulting bars? Deliciously chewy, caramelly, fruit-studded numbers that are deeply, deeply satisfying. If you need them to be nut-free too (hello school lunches!), you can easily swap the almonds for pepitas (pumpkin seeds).

Apricot, Almond & Coconut Muesli Bars

MAKES ONE 20 CM (8 INCH) SQUARE SLICE (12 PIECES)

100 g (3½ oz) unsalted butter

150 g (5½ oz) golden syrup (light treacle)

110 g (3¾ oz) caster (superfine) sugar

1 teaspoon vanilla bean paste

200 g (7 oz) rolled (porridge) oats

40 g (1½ oz) shredded coconut

40 g (1½ oz) desiccated coconut

2 teaspoons ground cinnamon

80 g (2¾ oz) almonds

120 g (4¼ oz) dried apricots, roughly chopped

¼ teaspoon fine sea salt

Preheat the oven to 140°C (275°F) fan-forced and line a 20 cm (8 inch) square cake tin with baking paper, leaving enough paper overhanging to help lift the cooked slice out of the tin.

Place the butter, golden syrup and sugar in a saucepan over low heat and cook, stirring often, until the butter has melted and the sugar has dissolved. Stir in the vanilla and set aside.

In a large mixing bowl, place the rolled oats, shredded and desiccated coconut, ground cinnamon, almonds, dried apricots and salt. Stir to combine, before making a well in the centre and pouring in the melted butter and golden syrup mixture. Mix well, making sure to coat all the dry ingredients. Spoon into the prepared tin and press out firmly into an even layer using an offset palette knife or the bottom of a glass.

Bake in the preheated oven for 30–40 minutes or until the slice is toasty brown all over and starting to caramelise around the edges. The slice will still be soft when you remove it from the oven, but will firm up as it cools. Use an offset palette knife or the bottom of a glass to compress the slice again while it's still warm, then allow it to cool completely in the tin. When cool, lift the slice out and use a large sharp knife to slice into 12 bars.

STORE & SHARE *Muesli bars keep happily in an airtight container in a cool place for up to a week. They also travel well – to picnics, in lunchboxes or well wrapped, in the post! (See page 9 for tips on packing and posting baked goods.)*

These are the brownies of my dreams; a crackly, meringue-like top and gooey, intensely chocolatey interior (studded with nuggets of white chocolate for good measure). They remain my children's most requested bake. Some afternoons, when bedtime still seems like a distant dream, we make a batch and, when they're cooked, I plonk the kids in the bath, chunks of still-warm brownie in their hands. Water and chocolate therapy in one. And, even better, it doesn't matter one bit if the crumbs go everywhere and their faces end up covered in chocolate. I just rinse the kids off and let the chocolate crumbs and the remains of the never-ending day wash right down the plug-hole. Heaven!

Sour Cream Brownies

MAKES ONE 20 CM (8 INCH) SQUARE BROWNIE (12 PIECES)

150 g (5½ oz) unsalted butter, cubed

250 g (9 oz) dark chocolate (45–55% cocoa solids), roughly chopped

3 eggs

250 g (9 oz) caster (superfine) sugar

100 g (3½ oz) plain (all-purpose) flour

¼ teaspoon fine sea salt

2 tablespoons (20 g/¾ oz) Dutch-process (unsweetened) cocoa powder

150 g (5 oz) sour cream

2 teaspoons vanilla bean paste

100 g (3½ oz) white chocolate, roughly chopped

Preheat the oven to 160°C (325°F) fan-forced and line the base and sides of a 20 cm (8 inch) square cake tin with baking paper, leaving enough paper overhanging to help lift the cooked brownie out of the tin.

Place the butter, then the dark chocolate in a medium saucepan and place over very low heat, stirring often so the chocolate doesn't catch on the bottom of the pan. You can also do this in a double boiler if you prefer, but I find that as long as the heat is very low and you stir the mixture often, this method works just fine! Continue to stir until the chocolate and butter have melted and you have a gloriously glossy, warm chocolate puddle. Remove from the heat and allow to cool slightly while you whisk the eggs.

Place the eggs and sugar in the bowl of a stand mixer with a whisk attachment and whisk on medium–high speed until the mixture is thick and pale, 3–5 minutes. While the eggs and sugar are whisking, place the plain flour, salt and cocoa powder in a bowl and mix well. Set aside.

In a separate small bowl, stir the sour cream until smooth, then use a hand whisk to mix it into the warm chocolate mixture, along with the vanilla. Gently fold the chocolatey sour cream mixture into the whisked eggs and sugar. When the dark chocolate mixture is almost all folded through, sift the flour, salt and cocoa over the top, and gently fold this in too. Lastly, stir in the white chocolate pieces. Pour the batter in the prepared tin, smoothing the top with a spatula and tapping the tin gently on the bench a few times to remove any large air bubbles. →

Bake in the preheated oven for 35–40 minutes or until the surface is shiny and set, but the brownie is still a little wobbly underneath when the tin is jiggled. Allow to cool completely in the tin (if you can wait!) before lifting it out and slicing into pieces. The brownie will slice much better when cold, but, as I prefer a warm brownie, I forgo neat slices in favour of a quicker return! Either way, a large, hot sharp knife is the way to go.

Serve the brownies at room temperature with a cup of tea or while taking a lovely hot bath, or warm with a little puddle of cream and some berries for a very satisfactory dessert.

STORE & SHARE *Any left-over brownies will keep happily in an airtight container in the fridge for up to a week – and, in my experience, friends or teachers are always grateful for a brownie or two, wrapped up and handed over at school pickup!*

The flowers on the one cosmos plant that I saved from the slugs are nodding happily at me as I put together this late-summer slice – the very last of the peaches and plump red raspberries fanned across pistachio frangipane. It's satisfyingly pretty, and also just plain satisfying to carefully slice and arrange the fruit. A little pocket of meditation and culinary joy. I'll make this slice again in the coming months and top it with firm, tart plums and autumn blackberries which are, incidentally, also very good. But for now, I'm savouring the last little rays of summer, one slice at a time.

Raspberry & Peach Late-summer Slice

——————— MAKES ONE 20 X 30 CM (8 X 12 INCH) SLICE (15 PIECES) ———————

BASE

80 g (2¾ oz) pistachio kernels
150 g (5½ oz) plain (all-purpose) flour
80 g (2¾ oz) caster (superfine) sugar
⅛ teaspoon fine sea salt
125 g (4½ oz) unsalted butter, melted and cooled

FRANGIPANE

80 g (2¾ oz) pistachio kernels
125 g (4½ oz) unsalted butter, softened
110 g (3¾ oz) caster (superfine) sugar
1 teaspoon vanilla bean paste
2 eggs
80 g (2¾ oz) almond meal
50 g (1¾ oz) plain (all-purpose) flour
⅛ teaspoon fine sea salt
1 teaspoon rosewater

Ingredients continued over page

Line the base and sides of a 20 x 30 cm (8 x 12 inch) slice (slab) or lamington tin with baking paper, leaving enough paper overhanging to help lift the cooked slice out of the tin.

First, in a small food processor, blitz the pistachio kernels (both the 80 g/2¾ oz for the base, and the 80 g/2¾ oz for the frangipane) until fine.

Next, make the base for the slice by combining the flour, 80 g (2¾ oz) of the ground pistachios (setting the other 80 g/2¾ oz aside for the frangipane), the sugar and salt in a mixing bowl. Make a well in the centre and pour in the melted butter. Mix with a wooden spoon or spatula until combined. Tip the mixture into the base of your prepared tin and press it out into an even layer using an offset palette knife or the bottom of a glass. Place the tin in the fridge (or freezer if you have space), until well chilled and firm.

While the base is chilling, preheat the oven to 170°C (325°F) fan-forced.

When firm, prick the base all over with a fork and bake in the preheated oven for 15–20 minutes or until golden brown and smelling deliciously toasty. Allow to cool slightly while you make the frangipane.

Lower the oven temperature to 160°C (325°F) fan-forced. In the bowl of a stand mixer with a paddle attachment, cream the butter, caster sugar and vanilla until light and fluffy. →

TOPPING

3 peaches, ripe but firm

125 g (4½ oz) fresh raspberries

**2 tablespoons good peach or
apricot jam**

1 teaspoon rosewater

**1 tablespoon pistachio kernels
roughly chopped**

Add the eggs, one at a time, beating well after each addition. Stir in the remaining ground pistachios and the almond meal, followed by the flour, salt and rosewater, and beat for a minute or so until the mixture is light.

Top the cooked base with the frangipane and use a spatula to smooth it out into an even layer. Cut the peaches into quarters, discarding the pits. Slice the peach quarters into thin slices and fan them out over the surface of the slice, then nestle the raspberries into the batter between the peach slices. Bake in the preheated oven for 40–50 minutes, or until the frangipane is golden and cooked through.

Heat the peach or apricot jam until bubbling (I do this in a small bowl in the microwave), then add the rosewater and stir it through. Once the slice is cooked, use a pastry brush to gently glaze the top of the slice with the hot jam mixture, until beautifully shiny. Scatter over the chopped pistachios. Allow the slice to cool completely in the tin before lifting it out and slicing into squares with a sharp knife.

STORE & SHARE *Best eaten on the day it is baked, this slice is particularly fine picnic fare! Store any leftovers in an airtight container in the fridge for up to 3 days, returning to room temperature before serving.*

Sweet, sticky and delicious. An ode to the old-fashioned caramel slice (millionaire's shortbread) of my childhood, but a little more grown up. She has the added warmth and bite of fresh ginger, which works beautifully as a foil for the sweet caramel, and the crunch of toasted pecans – all set on a sturdy, oaty, coconutty base (a good foundation is essential, no?). She's definitely a keeper this one!

Pecan, Caramel & Ginger Bars

MAKES ONE 20 CM (8 INCH) SQUARE SLICE (18 PIECES)

BASE
75 g (2½ oz) plain (all-purpose) flour
¼ teaspoon bicarbonate of soda (baking soda)
80 g (2¾ oz) quick oats
40 g (1½ oz) desiccated coconut
80 g (2¾ oz) golden (raw) caster (superfine) sugar
¼ teaspoon fine sea salt
80 g (2¾ oz) unsalted butter, melted and cooled
1 tablespoon pure maple syrup
1 teaspoon vanilla bean paste
65 g (2½ oz) pecans

CARAMEL
395 g (13¾ oz) tinned sweetened condensed milk
80 g (2¾ oz) unsalted butter, cubed
60 ml (2 fl oz) pure maple syrup

Ingredients continued over page

Line the base and sides of a 20 cm (8 inch) square cake tin with baking paper, leaving enough paper overhanging to help lift the cooked slice out of the tin.

First, make the base by placing the flour, bicarbonate of soda, oats, coconut, sugar and salt in a mixing bowl. Mix to combine, before making a well in the centre of the dry ingredients. Pour in the melted butter, maple syrup and vanilla and use a wooden spoon to mix well. Tip the rubbly mixture into the base of your prepared tin and press it out firmly into an even layer using an offset palette knife or the bottom of a glass. Place the tin in the fridge (or freezer if you have space), until well chilled and firm.

While the base is chilling, preheat the oven to 150°C (300°F) fan-forced.

When the base is firm, bake in the preheated oven for 20–25 minutes or until golden brown and smelling deliciously toasty. Top the biscuit base with 65 g (2½ oz) pecans and return to the oven for another 5 minutes. Remove from the oven and set aside to cool while you make the caramel topping.

Place the sweetened condensed milk, butter, maple syrup and sugar in a small saucepan. Place over medium–low heat and stir until the butter has melted and the sugar has dissolved. →

55 g (2 oz) light brown sugar

2 teaspoons peeled and
   finely diced fresh ginger

135 g (4¾ oz) pecans

Flaky sea salt, to sprinkle

Bring the mixture to a gentle boil, then turn the heat down to low and continue to cook, stirring with a spatula or whisk to prevent it from burning on the bottom, for 10–12 minutes or until the caramel has thickened slightly and is a lovely deep beige colour.

Remove from the heat and stir in the diced ginger. Pour the caramel carefully over the biscuit base and toasted pecans, smoothing it out into an even layer with a spatula.

Arrange the remaining pecans on top, sprinkle with flaky sea salt and return the slice to the oven for a further 15–18 minutes, or until the caramel is a shade darker and bubbling around the edges.

Allow the slice to cool to room temperature before placing the tin in the fridge to chill for a couple of hours. This makes it much easier to slice neatly! Use the extra baking paper to lift it out of the tin. Slice into pieces using a large, hot sharp knife.

STORE & SHARE *This slice keeps well in an airtight container somewhere cool for up to a week. As it keeps so well, this is the perfect bake to have on hand in case friends drop by; meaning that, happily, a little caramel-care is never too far away!*

Baked quince is quite possibly one of my favourite things. Not only does the baking of it perfume your house with the most deliciously autumnal smell (reason alone to make it), but you are also left with beautiful, ruby-hued wedges of fruit with which to top cakes and porridge! Or to nestle into a creamy ricotta filling and top with burnt butter crumble, as in this quince slice. It is really rather wonderful – the crimson quince slices peeking coyly out from beneath the rubbly, golden topping.

When quinces are not in season, you can substitute them with a batch of Marmalade Baked Rhubarb (page 213) and swap the Plum & Star Anise Jam for Strawberry & Rhubarb Jam (page 211). This is also a very fine combination.

Quince & Ricotta Crumble Squares

MAKES ONE 20 X 30 CM (8 X 12 INCH) SLICE (15 PIECES)

CRUMBLE AND BASE

400 g (14 oz) plain (all-purpose) flour
½ teaspoon ground cinnamon
180 g (6½ oz) caster (superfine) sugar
¼ teaspoon fine sea salt
250 g (9 oz) unsalted butter, cubed

FILLING

300 g (10½ oz) fresh ricotta, drained
250 g (9 oz) cream cheese, at room temperature
110 g (3¾ oz) caster (superfine) sugar
1½ teaspoons vanilla bean paste
1 egg
100 g (3½ oz) Plum & Star Anise Jam (page 207), or other good red jam

Ingredients continued over page

Line the base and sides of a 20 x 30 cm (8 x 12 inch) slice (slab) or lamington tin with baking paper, leaving enough paper overhanging to help lift the cooked slice out of the tin.

First, start the crumble and base mixture by placing the flour, cinnamon, sugar and salt in a large mixing bowl, using a hand whisk to combine.

Next, brown the butter by placing it in a saucepan over medium heat. Cook the butter, swirling the pan occasionally, until it has melted and starts to bubble rapidly. Once the bubbles slow and the butter starts to foam, watch carefully. When small brown flecks appear at the bottom of the pan, quickly remove from the heat. Pour the browned butter over the dry ingredients and stir to a soft, chunky crumble using a fork.

Spoon about two-thirds of the mixture into the base of the prepared tin and press it out into an even layer using an offset palette knife or the bottom of a glass. Place the tin in the fridge (or freezer if you have space), until well chilled and firm. Place the remaining crumble mixture in the fridge to chill too – this will be sprinkled on top of the slice later.

While the base is chilling, preheat the oven to 170°C (325°F) fan-forced.

When chilled, prick the base all over with a fork and bake in the preheated oven for 20–25 minutes or until it is just starting to colour and smell deliciously toasty. Remove from the oven and set aside to cool slightly while you make the ricotta filling. →

**½ quantity Baked Quince
(page 216), or Marmalade
Baked Rhubarb (page 213)**

Place the ricotta, cream cheese, sugar, vanilla and egg in the bowl of a stand mixer with a paddle attachment and mix thoroughly to combine. Pour the ricotta mixture on top of the cooked base, smoothing it out into an even layer with a spatula. Remove any star anise pieces from the plum jam before dolloping it (or other jam of choice) over the surface of the ricotta, then nestle the baked quince slices (or baked rhubarb) into the mixture. Sprinkle over the reserved crumble topping.

Bake in the preheated oven for 30–35 minutes or until the ricotta filling is set and the crumble topping is just starting to colour.

Allow the slice to cool to room temperature in the tin before placing the whole tray in the fridge to chill for a couple of hours. Once cold, slice into squares and serve cold or at room temperature.

 STORE & SHARE *Store any leftovers in an airtight container in the fridge, to share with family and friends, within 2–3 days.*

File this one under 'lunchbox staples' and 'stupendously easy' and thank me later! I'm not quite sure why it has taken me so long to rediscover the childhood bake-sale favourite that is chocolate coconut slice, but golly, I'm glad I have. So are my kids! This melt-and-mix slice is all chewy coconut and cocoa, and with a simple chocolate icing it hits the right notes. I'm rather partial to it topped with sprinkles, but if you're going for a more refined aesthetic, by all means go with flaked coconut, as it does look rather chic.

A Very Easy Chocolate Coconut Slice

MAKES ONE 20 CM (8 INCH) SQUARE SLICE (16 PIECES)

BASE

150 g (5½ oz) self-raising flour

3 tablespoons (30 g/1 oz) Dutch-process (unsweetened) cocoa powder, sifted

80 g (2¾ oz) desiccated coconut

220 g (7¾ oz) caster (superfine) sugar

¼ teaspoon fine sea salt

125 g (4½ oz) unsalted butter, melted and cooled

1 egg, lightly beaten

ICING (FROSTING)

160 g (5½ oz) icing (confectioners') sugar mixture

2 tablespoons (20 g/¾ oz) Dutch-process (unsweetened) cocoa powder, sifted

20 g (¾ oz) unsalted butter

1½ tablespoons (30 ml/1 fl oz) full-cream (whole) milk, hot

Flaked coconut, or sprinkles, to top (optional)

Preheat the oven to 170°C (325°F) fan-forced and line the base and sides of a 20 cm (8 inch) square cake tin with baking paper, leaving enough paper overhanging to help lift the cooked slice out of the tin.

Place the flour, cocoa, desiccated coconut, caster sugar and salt in a mixing bowl and use a hand whisk to combine. Make a well in the centre of the dry ingredients and pour in the melted butter and egg. Use a wooden spoon or spatula to mix to a soft dough.

Spoon the mixture into the prepared tin, smoothing it out to an even layer using an offset palette knife or the bottom of a glass. Bake in the preheated oven for 20–25 minutes or until the surface is set, the slice is smelling lovely and chocolatey, and only a few damp crumbs cling to a skewer when the slice is tested. Allow to cool completely in the tin.

When the slice is cool, make the icing by combining the icing sugar mixture and cocoa powder in a mixing bowl. Melt the butter in the hot milk, then add the mixture to the bowl with the icing sugar and cocoa. Stir to a smooth chocolatey paste before spreading it evenly over the top of the slice. Sprinkle with flaked coconut or sprinkles (if using) and allow the icing to set before slicing into squares using a large sharp knife.

STORE & SHARE *This slice keeps happily in an airtight container at room temperature for 4–5 days and is a rather excellent lunchbox addition!*

Any slice crowned with a halo of crisp meringue is a good idea in my book. Even better when the meringue is delicately scented with orange blossom and hides a layer of tart Roast Apricot Jam (page 206). And, when built on a sunny-yellow polenta biscuit base, you've really hit dream territory, I think! Close your eyes and you could almost imagine yourself in a tiny seaside village on the Mediterranean coast, orange blossom tingling on the breeze. Ah, it's a nice dream, isn't it? Let's travel, vicariously. If you don't have any Roast Apricot Jam on hand, use a good-quality store-bought jam – just make sure it's nice and tart.

Orange Blossom & Apricot Jam Slice

MAKES ONE 20 X 30 CM (8 X 12 INCH) SLICE (15 PIECES)

BASE

125 g (4½ oz) unsalted butter, softened
165 g (5¾ oz) caster (superfine) sugar
Finely grated zest of ½ orange
1 teaspoon vanilla bean paste
3 egg yolks
185 g (6½ oz) plain (all-purpose) flour
1 teaspoon baking powder
80 g (2¾ oz) fine polenta
⅛ teaspoon fine sea salt
320 g (11¼ oz) Roast Apricot Jam (page 206)

MERINGUE

3 egg whites
Pinch of fine sea salt
¼ teaspoon cream of tartar
165 g (5¾ oz) caster (superfine) sugar
1 teaspoon orange blossom water

Line the base and sides of a 20 x 30 cm (8 x 12 inch) slice (slab) or lamington tin with baking paper, leaving enough paper overhanging to help lift the cooked slice out of the tin.

In the bowl of a stand mixer with a paddle attachment, cream the butter, sugar, orange zest and vanilla until light and fluffy. Add the egg yolks, beating well to incorporate.

Place the flour, baking powder, polenta and salt in a separate bowl and use a hand whisk to combine. Add the dry ingredients to the creamed butter mixture, stirring gently until combined.

Spoon the batter into the prepared tin, smoothing it out to an even layer using an offset palette knife. Place the tin in the fridge (or freezer if you have space), until well chilled and firm.

While the base is chilling, preheat the oven to 170°C (325°F) fan-forced.

When chilled, prick the base all over with a fork and bake in the preheated oven for 25–30 minutes or until the surface is set and the base smells lovely and toasty. Turn the oven down to 150°C (300°F) fan-forced and allow the base to cool while you make the meringue topping.

Place the egg whites, salt and cream of tartar in the clean bowl of a stand mixer with a whisk attachment and whisk until soft peaks form. Add the sugar, 1 tablespoon at a time, beating well after each addition. →

Once all the sugar has been added, scrape down the side of the bowl and continue to whisk on medium–high speed until all the sugar has dissolved and the meringue is thick and glossy. Add the orange blossom water and fold it through.

Spread the apricot jam over the cooked slice base, then gently spoon the meringue on top, smoothing and swirling it out with a palette knife. Bake in the preheated oven for 30–35 minutes or until the surface of the meringue is crisp and a beautiful dusky beige colour. Allow the slice to cool completely in the tin before gently lifting it out and slicing with a large sharp knife.

STORE & SHARE *This slice is best eaten on the day it is made, while the meringue is crisp, but any leftovers can be stored in an airtight container somewhere cool for up to 2 days.*

The sweet scent of caramelised sugar is in the air and our hair smells honeyed and sweet. The kitchen is a mess; a trail of biscuit crumbs creeps across the table and there's icing on the floor. But the biscuit tin is full and so are we. And there is the promise of treats tucked away for lunchboxes and rainy days, or maybe just for tomorrow.

Speaking of comfort and care, and sugar-crusted 'hellos', homemade biscuits really are pure magic. It's something to do with simple, nostalgic delight and the slightly wonky, squidgy shapes made by small hands shaping dough. Standing on a stool making biscuits in my parents' kitchen is one of my earliest baking memories, and one which I hope will be added to my children's memory banks too.

Biscuit Crumbs, Coconut & Chocolate Kisses

Now, I like a good plain biscuit almost as much as I do a plain cake, and jam drops would have to be one of the finest plain biscuits around. They were one of the first biscuits that I learnt to bake – and if any biscuits were designed to be made by children, it would have to be jam drops! For they are positively clamouring to be shaped by eager little hands and enthusiastically poked at to make way for a (slightly too big) spoonful of jam. What they lack in finesse they surely make up for in charm?

Coconut Jam Drops

MAKES ABOUT 24 BISCUITS

125 g (4½ oz) unsalted butter, softened

55 g (2 oz) caster (superfine) sugar

1 teaspoon vanilla bean paste

110 g (3¾ oz) plain (all-purpose) flour

40 g (1½ oz) cornflour (cornstarch)

½ teaspoon baking powder

40 g (1½ oz) desiccated coconut

⅛ teaspoon fine sea salt

160 g (5½ oz) Strawberry & Rhubarb Jam (page 211), Roast Apricot Jam (page 206) or Plum & Star Anise Jam (page 207), or good-quality store-bought jam

In the bowl of a stand mixer with a paddle attachment, cream the butter, sugar and vanilla until light and fluffy. Place the flour, cornflour, baking powder, coconut and salt in a separate bowl and use a hand whisk to combine. Add to the creamed butter mixture and stir gently until a soft dough forms. Let the dough rest in the bowl somewhere cool for half an hour (in the fridge if the weather is very hot).

While the dough is resting, preheat the oven to 160°C (325°F) fan-forced and line two baking trays with baking paper.

Use your hands to roll the dough into balls (about 2 teaspoons of dough per ball) and place on the baking trays, leaving a little space between the biscuits as they will spread while cooking. Make an indent in the centre of each biscuit using your thumb, or the back of a ½ teaspoon measure, and fill with a small spoonful of jam. Bake the biscuits in the preheated oven for 12 minutes or until they are just starting to colour. Remove the trays from the oven and top up the jam in each biscuit with another little spoonful. Return to the oven for a further 3–5 minutes, until the biscuits are golden and the jam has spread.

Remove the trays from the oven. Cool the biscuits on the trays for 10 minutes before transferring to a wire rack to cool completely.

STORE & SHARE *Store any left-over biscuits in an airtight container at room temperature for 2–3 days. The biscuits may soften when stored if the weather is humid, but can be crisped by baking again for 10 minutes at 150°C (300°F) fan-forced.*

Some days require a little chocolate cheer, don't they? The days when we're all a little frazzled, a little tired, or just downright cranky. I find chocolate biscuits usually help. Or, at the very least, they take the edge off! These chocolatey, nutty thumbprints have the added bonus of being very easy to make, and are useful for keeping little hands occupied. They also keep very well and are particularly heavenly with a last cup of tea once the rest of the house is asleep. Happily, they are gluten-free, which (irrationally I know), always makes me think I can eat double, guilt-free. But when filled with chocolate hazelnut spread, they are rather hard to resist.

Chocolate Hazelnut Thumbprints

MAKES ABOUT 28 BISCUITS * GLUTEN FREE

60 g (2¼ oz) roasted hazelnuts, skins removed (see page 9)
125 g (4½ oz) unsalted butter, softened
80 g (2¾ oz) pure icing (confectioners') sugar, sifted
1 teaspoon vanilla bean paste
100 g (3½ oz) gluten-free cornflour (cornstarch)
2 tablespoons (20 g/¾ oz) Dutch-process (unsweetened) cocoa powder, sifted
80 g (2¾ oz) white rice flour
¼ teaspoon fine sea salt
160 g (5½ oz) store-bought chocolate hazelnut spread, to fill

Preheat the oven to 150°C (300°F) fan-forced and line two baking trays with baking paper. Place the hazelnuts in a small blender and blitz until fine. Set aside.

In the bowl of a stand mixer with a paddle attachment, cream the butter, sugar and vanilla until light and fluffy. Place the cornflour, cocoa, rice flour, ground hazelnuts and salt in a separate mixing bowl and use a hand whisk to combine. Add the dry ingredients to the creamed butter mixture, mixing on low speed and scraping down the side of the bowl once, until the dough comes together.

Use your hands to roll the dough into balls (about 2 teaspoons of dough per ball), then place on the prepared trays, leaving a little space between the biscuits as they will spread while cooking. Use your thumb, or the back of a rounded ½ teaspoon measure, to press a hole in the centre of each biscuit. Don't worry if the biscuits crack a little around the edges – we're going for rustic joy here, not perfection! Place the biscuits in the preheated oven and bake for 15 minutes.

Remove the trays from the oven and use the back of a 1 teaspoon measuring spoon to gently press the holes back into the centres of the biscuits, taking care not to break them apart (they may crack slightly, but that is fine). Fill the hot biscuits with a dollop of the chocolate hazelnut spread. Allow the biscuits to cool completely on the trays before serving or storing.

STORE & SHARE *Store for up to a week in an airtight container.*

Delightfully unassuming, these biscuits may sound (and look) rather unremarkable – but can I just say, in the middle of a busy day, one of these with a cup of tea makes a huge difference. I sighed audibly when I first ate one, and that is always a very good sign. Delicately short and buttery, with just enough zing from the lemon zest, these biscuits keep exceptionally well. And surely nothing is so reassuring as a full biscuit tin?

Do take the time to rub the lemon zest into the sugar well before you cream it with the butter – not only is it thoroughly therapeutic, but it really does give the shortbread a more intense lemon flavour.

Very Short Lemon Shortbread

MAKES ABOUT 20 BISCUITS

110 g (3¾ oz) caster (superfine) sugar, plus extra to sprinkle
Finely grated zest of 1 lemon
250 g (9 oz) unsalted butter, softened
1 teaspoon vanilla bean paste
200 g (7 oz) plain (all-purpose) flour
½ teaspoon baking powder
100 g (3½ oz) white rice flour
¼ teaspoon fine sea salt

First, place the sugar and lemon zest in the bowl of a stand mixer and use your fingertips to rub the zest through the sugar until fragrant. Add the butter and vanilla and, using the paddle attachment, beat until light and fluffy.

Place the plain flour, baking powder, rice flour and salt in a separate bowl and use a hand whisk to combine. Add the dry ingredients to the creamed butter mixture, stirring gently until the dough just comes together. Tip the soft mixture out onto a sheet of baking paper and use your hands to pat it out slightly to flatten. Place another sheet of baking paper on top and roll the dough out until it is about 8 mm (⅜ inch) thick. Place in the fridge for an hour or so, until it is firm enough to cut.

When the shortbread is firm, preheat the oven to 140°C (275°F) fan-forced and line two baking trays with baking paper.

Use a 6 cm (2½ inch) round cutter to cut out 20 biscuits, re-rolling the dough as necessary. Place the biscuits on the prepared trays, leaving a little space between them as they will spread while cooking. Sprinkle the biscuits with a little extra caster sugar, then bake for 20–25 minutes or until the shortbread is just starting to colour. Remove the biscuits from the oven and sprinkle with a little more caster sugar. Allow the shortbread to cool completely on the trays before eating, or storing.

STORE & SHARE *Store the shortbread in an airtight container at room temperature for up to a month. The perfect stand-by sweet treat!*

Whisper-light and deliberately tiny, these sugary little gems are just begging to be eaten! I like mine delicately scented with rosewater and strawberry, or with the sweet citrus flavour of orange blossom water. But they are also very good just as they are, in all their vanillary-glory, or with the sweet, grassy flavour of matcha green tea (better than I've made it sound, I promise!). Below you will find my base vanilla meringue recipe, followed by my favourite flavour variations.

Baby Meringues

MAKES ABOUT 24 BITE-SIZED MERINGUES * GLUTEN FREE

3 egg whites (approximately 100 g/3½ oz)
180 g (6½ oz) caster (superfine) sugar
1 teaspoon vanilla bean paste
Pinch of fine sea salt

Combine the egg whites and sugar in a heatproof bowl set over a saucepan of gently simmering water, making sure the water does not touch the base of the bowl. Heat the mixture, stirring constantly with a rubber spatula, until it is warm and the sugar has dissolved, about 3–4 minutes. Remove the bowl from the heat and transfer the mixture to the bowl of a stand mixer with a whisk attachment. Whisk on medium speed for 2 minutes before increasing the speed to medium–high and whisking for a further 6–8 minutes or until the mixture has cooled and the meringue is glossy and holds firm peaks. Add the vanilla and salt and gently fold them through.

While the meringue mixture is whisking, preheat the oven to 110°C (225°F) fan-forced, and line two baking trays with baking paper. Dot a little meringue on the underside of each corner of the baking paper and use this to glue the paper to the trays.

Transfer the meringue mixture to a piping bag with a 1.5–2 cm (⅝–¾ inch) plain nozzle, and pipe small meringues (about 1 tablespoon per meringue) on the trays, leaving a little space between each. Alternatively, use two dessertspoons to spoon blobs of meringue free-form on the trays.

Place the trays in the preheated oven and immediately lower the temperature to 80°C (150°F) fan-forced. Bake the meringues for 60–75 minutes, or until they are crisp on the outside and lift off the baking paper easily. Turn the oven off and allow the meringues to cool in the oven with the door slightly ajar. →

Serve the meringues on their own, with a pot of tea or coffee or with a batch of Lemon Gems (page 94) for a decadent dessert.

STORE & SHARE *Store any left-over meringues in an airtight container for up to a week – and bring them out to serve on their own with tea or coffee when a tiny treat is in order.*

VARIATIONS

ROSE & STRAWBERRY Replace the vanilla bean paste with 1 teaspoon of rosewater and fold it through the meringue mixture, along with 10 g (¼ oz) of roughly crushed freeze-dried strawberries and the salt. Sprinkle the meringues with edible dried rose petals, or rose petal powder, before baking.

ORANGE BLOSSOM Replace the vanilla bean paste with 1 teaspoon of orange blossom water and fold it through the meringue mixture along with the salt. Top the meringues with chopped dried orange slices before baking.

MATCHA & VANILLA Sift 1 teaspoon of matcha green tea powder over the whipped meringue mixture and fold it through along with the vanilla bean paste and salt. Dust the meringues with a little extra matcha before baking.

I'm going to be honest here and confess that I have never been much fussed about chocolate chip cookies. Too often I've found them too sweet, too one-dimensional, to really be bothered with. I'd rather have a piece of cake. But my children are particularly fond of them and, to this end, I made it my mission to come up with a version that we all loved.

Enter this burnt butter and rye version – a happy intersection between childhood favourite and grown-up treat – the sweetness tempered by toasty burnt butter and nutty rye flour. Chocolate and rye is a combination that was first introduced to me by way of Gill Meller's beautiful book *Gather*. In it he has a recipe for chocolate rye brownies, and they are wonderful. Since then, my mind always turns to rye when the sweetness of chocolate is in need of mellowing.

Burnt Butter, Rye & Chocolate Chip Cookies

MAKES ABOUT 24 COOKIES

170 g (6 oz) unsalted butter, cubed
200 g (7 oz) rye flour
¼ teaspoon fine sea salt
1 teaspoon baking powder
110 g (3¾ oz) caster (superfine) sugar
140 g (5 oz) light brown sugar
150 g (5½ oz) dark chocolate (45–55% cocoa solids), roughly chopped
1 teaspoon vanilla bean paste
1 egg, lightly beaten
Sea salt flakes, to sprinkle (optional)

First, brown the butter by placing it in a saucepan over medium heat. Cook the butter, swirling the pan occasionally, until the butter has melted and starts to bubble rapidly. Once the bubbles slow and the butter starts to foam, watch carefully. When small brown flecks appear at the bottom of the pan, quickly remove from the heat and set the butter aside to cool.

When the butter has cooled, make the dough by placing the flour, salt, baking powder, caster sugar, brown sugar and chocolate in a large mixing bowl, stirring well to combine. Make a well in the centre of the dry ingredients and pour in the cooled browned butter, vanilla and beaten egg. Use a wooden spoon to bring the dough together. This dough takes a bit of mixing and will look a little dry to start off with, but don't worry, keep mixing and it will come together.

Roll tablespoonfuls of the dough into balls and flatten slightly, (or scoop up and shape portions of the dough using a 1 tablespoon ice cream scoop) and place them on the trays, leaving space between the cookies as they will spread while cooking. Place in the fridge to chill for at least 1 hour (or up to 2 days). This chilling time is boring, I know, but it gives the butter time to solidify and the flour time to hydrate, which will give a better texture and flavour to your cookies. →

(If you are not planning to bake your cookies the same day, you can place the dough balls in an airtight container, separated by sheets of baking paper, so you don't have baking trays in your fridge taking up all the space! Just place the dough balls on the baking trays when ready to bake.)

When ready to bake the cookies, preheat the oven to 150°C (300°F) fan-forced.

Bake the cookies for 10 minutes. Take the trays out of the oven and, being careful not to burn yourself or tip the biscuits off the tray, drop the tray once or twice onto the bench. This helps flatten the domed middle of the cookies, encouraging them to spread evenly. Sprinkle the tops with a little sea salt if you like, then return them to the oven for a further 5–7 minutes or until the cookies have spread and are golden brown around the edges (5 minutes will give you a bit of chew in the middle, while 7 minutes will give you a crisper cookie).

The cookies will be soft when you take them out of the oven, but will firm up as they cool. Allow to cool on the tray for at least 10 minutes before digging in!

STORE & SHARE *Store the cookies in an airtight container at room temperature for up to a week. These cookies are also wonderful as part of a care package, carefully packed up (and even posted) for a cheering doorstep delivery. (See page 9 for tips on packing and posting baked goods.)*

Melting moments, and the passionfruit variety in particular, have long been my biscuit of choice. Good ones are hard to come by but, when you do, they are like gold. I have exceptionally fond memories of the care packages my mum sent me after I had my first child, as they invariably included a bundle or two of bite-sized melting moments. I will always remember that special, tired time – cup of tea and melting moment in hand, and Olive with a sprinkling of biscuit crumbs on her dear little head.

Passionfruit & Citrus Melting Moments

MAKES ABOUT 20 FILLED BISCUITS

BISCUITS

250 g (9 oz) unsalted butter, softened

80 g (2¾ oz) icing (confectioners') sugar mixture

Finely grated zest of 1 lemon, 1 lime or ½ orange

1 teaspoon vanilla bean paste

225 g (8 oz) plain (all-purpose) flour

½ teaspoon baking powder

100 g (3½ oz) custard powder

¼ teaspoon fine sea salt

PASSIONFRUIT BUTTERCREAM

100 g (3½ oz) unsalted butter, softened

200 g (7 oz) icing (confectioners') sugar mixture

1½ tablespoons fresh passionfruit pulp

1 teaspoon lemon, lime or orange juice

For the biscuits, place the butter, sugar, zest and vanilla in the bowl of a stand mixer with a paddle attachment and beat until light and fluffy.

In a separate mixing bowl, place the flour, baking powder, custard powder and salt and use a hand whisk to combine. Add the dry ingredients to the creamed butter and sugar, mixing briefly to a soft dough. Set the dough aside in the bowl for 15–30 minutes somewhere cool (in the fridge if it is hot) to firm up a little before shaping.

While the dough is resting, preheat the oven to 150°C (300°F) fan-forced and line two baking sheets with baking paper.

When the dough has rested, use your hands to roll it into balls (about 2 teaspoons of dough per ball). Place the balls on the trays, spaced out a little as they will spread while cooking, and flatten them slightly with the back of a fork. Bake in the preheated oven for 14–18 minutes or until the biscuits are cooked and just starting to colour. Allow the biscuits to cool on the trays for 10 minutes before transferring to a wire rack to cool completely before filling.

While the biscuits are cooling, make the passionfruit buttercream by placing all the ingredients in the bowl of a stand mixer with a paddle attachment and beating until light and fluffy. Sandwich the biscuits together generously with passionfruit buttercream. Allow the filling to firm slightly before serving, or eat straightaway, buttercream squidging gleefully out the sides!

STORE & SHARE *Store for 4–5 days in an airtight container.*

Like a cross between a giant Anzac biscuit and an oaty digestive, these Burnt Butter Oat Bars are a favourite go-to in our house with a cup of tea. They are staggeringly simple and wholesomely delicious in equal measure. I like mine sans chocolate, but my kids and husband are not convinced – they prefer a slick of chocolate and a sprinkle of salt. You choose your own adventure!

Burnt Butter Oat Bars

MAKES ONE 20 X 30 CM (8 X 12 INCH) SLICE (20 PIECES)

150 g (5½ oz) unsalted butter, cubed

1 tablespoon golden syrup (light treacle)

1 teaspoon vanilla bean paste

100 g (3½ oz) white spelt flour

½ teaspoon bicarbonate of soda (baking soda)

120 g (4¼ oz) quick oats

60 g (2¼ oz) desiccated coconut

110 g (3¾ oz) golden (raw) caster (superfine) sugar

¼ teaspoon fine sea salt

180 g (6½ oz) chocolate of your choice, melted (optional)

Flaky sea salt, to sprinkle (optional)

Line the base and sides of a 20 x 30 cm (8 x 12 inch) slice (slab) or lamington tin with baking paper, leaving enough paper overhanging to lift the cooked slice out of the tin.

First, brown the butter by placing it in a saucepan over medium heat. Cook the butter, swirling the pan occasionally, until the butter has melted and starts to bubble rapidly. Once the bubbles slow and the butter starts to foam, watch carefully. When small brown flecks appear at the bottom of the pan, quickly remove from the heat. Stir in the golden syrup and vanilla, being careful as the butter might spit, and set aside to cool slightly.

While the butter is cooling, place the flour, bicarbonate of soda, oats, coconut, sugar and fine sea salt in a separate bowl, and use a hand whisk to combine. Pour in the warm browned butter mixture and use a wooden spoon or spatula to mix well. Tip the rubbly mixture into the base of your tin and press it out firmly into an even layer using an offset palette knife or the bottom of a glass. Place the tin in the fridge (or freezer if you have space), until firm.

While the base is chilling, preheat the oven to 150°C (300°F) fan-forced.

When chilled, bake in the preheated oven for 20–25 minutes or until golden brown and smelling deliciously toasty. →

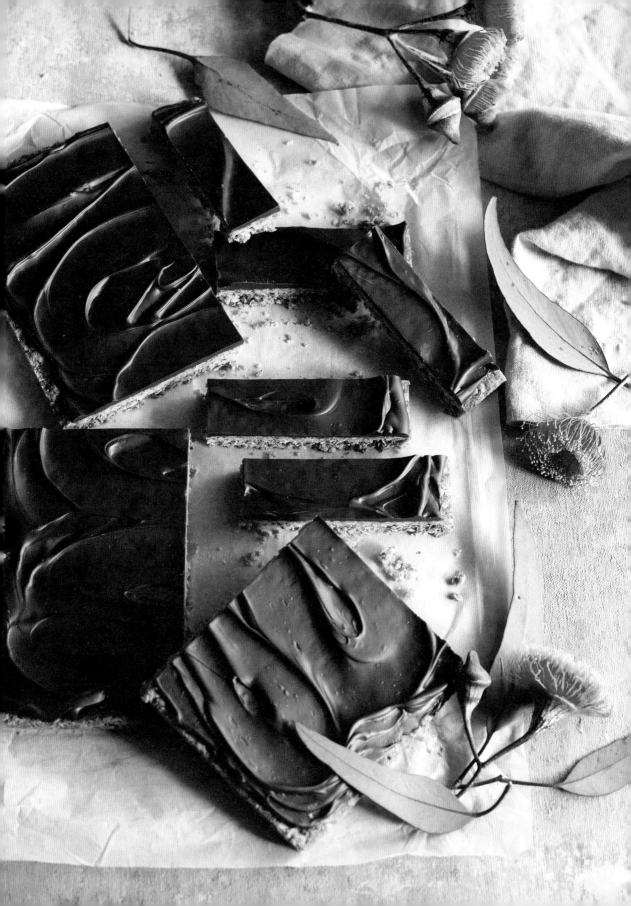

Leave the slice to cool completely before using the extra baking paper to lift it out of the tin. Pour the melted chocolate over the top (if using), spreading it out evenly across the surface.

Sprinkle with a little sea salt, if you like. Allow the chocolate to set, then slice into bars using a large, hot, sharp knife.

STORE & SHARE *The oat bars will keep happily in an airtight container at room temperature for up to a week. If they are coated in chocolate and the weather is warm, store them in the fridge. These oat bars travel very well and can even be posted (without the chocolate coating) as part of a care package. (See page 9 for tips on packing and posting baked goods.)*

The house and my hair smell sweetly chocolatey by the time I pull the trays of crackly, soft, cocoa-rich biscuits out of the oven. They'll harden up as they cool – as too, I hope, will my resolve not to eat them all straight from the tray, still warm and sticky. I want to sandwich them with zingy peppermint cream and save them for dessert. But I might have to eat just one now. For quality control, surely?

Now, I realise this might be a little polarising, but chocolate and mint is a real favourite of mine. When I was small, those thin after-dinner mint chocolates seemed impossibly chic (I did grow up in a country town!). These chewy, brownie-like biscuits sandwiched with soft peppermint cream filling, however, are a new favourite in our house. They feel particularly right with a cup of milky tea after dinner. After all, peppermint is excellent for digestion, yes?

Chewy Chocolate Mint Sandwiches

MAKES 10 FILLED BISCUITS

40 g (1½ oz) unsalted butter, cubed

150 g (5½ oz) dark chocolate (45–55% cocoa solids), roughly chopped

55 g (2 oz) caster (superfine) sugar

30 g (1 oz) light brown sugar

1 egg, plus 1 extra egg yolk

½ teaspoon vanilla bean paste

50 g (1¾ oz) plain (all-purpose) flour

½ teaspoon baking powder

2 teaspoons Dutch-process (unsweetened) cocoa powder, sifted

Pinch of fine sea salt

Flaky sea salt, to sprinkle (optional)

Ingredients continued over page

Preheat the oven to 160°C (325°F) fan-forced and line three baking trays with baking paper.

Place the butter and 100 g (3½ oz) of the chocolate in a small saucepan over very low heat. Cook, stirring often, until the chocolate and butter have melted, and you have a glorious smooth chocolate puddle. Set aside to cool slightly.

Meanwhile, place the caster sugar, brown sugar, egg and egg yolk in the bowl of a stand mixer with a whisk attachment and whisk until the mixture is pale, light and fluffy, 3–5 minutes. Fold through the melted chocolate mixture, along with the vanilla.

Place the flour, baking powder, cocoa and fine sea salt in a small bowl, and use a hand whisk to combine. Gently fold the dry ingredients through the chocolate mixture, followed by the remaining 50 g (1¾ oz) of the chopped chocolate. Use a teaspoon to drop generous teaspoonfuls of batter in neat blobs onto the trays, leaving plenty of room between the biscuits, as they will spread when baked. Sprinkle with a little flaky sea salt (if using), and bake in the preheated oven for 8–12 minutes, until the surface of the biscuits is crackly and set, but they are still soft underneath.

Leave the biscuits to cool completely on the trays. →

PEPPERMINT CREAM FILLING

250 g (9 oz) icing (confectioners')
   sugar mixture

¼ teaspoon peppermint extract

2 tablespoons full-cream (whole)
   milk

When the biscuits are cool, make the peppermint filling by placing the sugar in a mixing bowl. Add the peppermint extract to the bowl, along with 1½ tablespoons of the milk. Mix to a smooth, thick, spreadable paste, adding the remaining ½ tablespoon of milk, little by little, if necessary. Taste the mixture and add another drop of peppermint extract if you think it needs it. Gently sandwich the biscuits together with about 2 teaspoons of peppermint cream and serve them with a big pot of something hot.

STORE & SHARE *Store any left-over biscuits in an airtight container somewhere cool for up to a week, or win some new friends by sharing a few!*

Bake these cookies for their glorious colour palette alone. But then, really do eat them, because they are very delicious too! Their lightly floral, fruity flavour (hello freeze-dried strawberries and rosewater) is balanced by the herbaceously green notes of matcha tea and sweet vanilla. Pretty and delicious – my favourite combination! All these biscuits want for is an accompanying (bottomless) pot of tea and a quiet spot in which to hide away with an excellent book. May I suggest something by Jane Austen ...?

Matcha, Rose & Strawberry Cookies

MAKES ABOUT 22 COOKIES

180 g (6½ oz) unsalted butter, cubed

250 g (9 oz) plain (all-purpose) flour

½ teaspoon fine sea salt

1 teaspoon baking powder

220 g (7¾ oz) caster (superfine) sugar

1 egg, lightly beaten

½ teaspoon matcha green tea powder

½ teaspoon vanilla bean paste

1 teaspoon rosewater

1 teaspoon rose petal powder, or a few drops of pink food colouring

7 g (¼ oz) freeze-dried strawberries, roughly crushed

Preheat the oven to 150°C (300°F) fan-forced and line two baking trays with baking paper.

Brown the butter by placing it in a saucepan over medium heat. Swirl the pan occasionally, until the butter has melted and starts to bubble rapidly. Once the bubbles slow and the butter starts to foam, watch carefully. When small brown flecks appear at the bottom of the pan, quickly remove from the heat. Set aside to cool slightly.

Place the flour, salt, baking powder and sugar in a large mixing bowl and stir well to combine. Make a well in the centre of the dry ingredients and pour in the just-warm browned butter and the beaten egg. Use a wooden spoon to bring the dough together, then divide it in half and place in two separate bowls.

Sift the matcha powder onto the dough in one of the bowls and use your hands to mix it into the cookie dough, along with the vanilla. Add the rosewater, rose petal powder (or pink colouring), and crushed freeze-dried strawberries to the other bowl and use your hands to knead the ingredients evenly through the dough.

Pinch off about 2 teaspoons of the matcha dough and 2 teaspoons of the rose and strawberry dough and roll together into a ball, so that you have a marbled ball. Repeat with the remaining dough. Place the biscuits on the trays, flattening them a little and leaving space between them as they will spread while cooking. →

Bake the cookies in the preheated oven for 15–18 minutes
(15 minutes will give you a bit of chew in the middle of the biscuits,
while 18 minutes will give you a crisper biscuit).

The cookies will be soft when you take them out of the oven, but
will firm up as they cool. Allow to cool on the tray for at least 10 minutes
before transferring to a wire rack to cool completely before serving
– with a big cup of milky matcha tea perhaps?

STORE & SHARE *Store the cookies in an airtight container at
room temperature for up to a week – or wrap some up carefully
and drop off a bundle to a friend in need of a sugar-crusted hello!
(See page 9 for tips on packing and posting baked goods.)*

Meringues are the one bake that never fails to delight my children. They simply love them! And these little beauties, filled with chewy coconut and a swirl of dark chocolate, really are a joy to eat. Have them after dinner with a big pot of something hot for a little sweet treat – or go all out and serve them with a bowl of softly whipped cream and some fresh berries. Store the meringues in an airtight container for up to a week.

Chocolate Coconut Meringues

MAKES ABOUT 18 SMALL MERINGUES * GLUTEN FREE

4 egg whites (approximately 140 g/5 oz)

150 g (5½ oz) caster (superfine) sugar

110 g (3¾ oz) light brown sugar

¼ teaspoon cream of tartar

80 g (2¾ oz) desiccated coconut

Pinch of fine sea salt

50 g (1¾ oz) dark chocolate (45–55% cocoa solids), melted and cooled

Dutch-process (unsweetened) cocoa powder, to dust

Combine the egg whites, caster sugar, brown sugar and cream of tartar in a heatproof bowl set over a saucepan of gently simmering water, making sure the water does not touch the base of the bowl. Heat the mixture, stirring constantly with a rubber spatula, until the mixture is warm and the sugar has dissolved, about 3–4 minutes.

Remove the bowl from the heat and transfer the mixture to the bowl of a stand mixer with a whisk attachment. Whisk on medium speed for 2 minutes before increasing the speed to medium–high and whisking for a further 6–8 minutes, or until the mixture has cooled and the meringue is glossy and holds firm peaks.

While the meringues are whisking, preheat the oven to 110°C (225°F) fan-forced and line two baking trays with baking paper. Dot a little meringue on the underside of each corner of baking paper and use this to glue the paper to the trays.

Gently fold the desiccated coconut, along with the salt, through the meringue. Pour in the cooled melted chocolate and marble it through the mixture. Use a soup spoon to drop heaped spoonfuls of meringue onto the prepared trays, leaving room between the meringues. Dust the tops liberally with cocoa.

Place the trays in the preheated oven and immediately lower the oven temperature to 80°C (150°F) fan-forced. Bake for 60–75 minutes, or until the meringues are crisp on the outside and lift off the baking paper easily. Turn the oven off and allow the meringues to cool in the oven with the door slightly ajar.

This is my version of an Australian childhood favourite (and the queen of the assorted cream box), the Monte Carlo. Two coconutty, oaty, brown sugar biscuits sandwiched with vanilla buttercream and tart, red plum jam. Heaven in two squidgy, jammy bites! There really is no elegant way to eat these, just get them in your mouth as fast as you can! Although best eaten on the day they are filled, these biscuits will keep happily in an airtight container in a cool place for 2–3 days. Store them in the fridge if the weather is very warm.

Plum Jam Monte Carlos™

MAKES ABOUT 20 FILLED BISCUITS

185 g (6½ oz) unsalted butter, softened

110 g (3¾ oz) light brown sugar

1 teaspoon vanilla bean paste

1 tablespoon (30 g/1 oz) golden syrup (light treacle)

1 egg, lightly beaten

225 g (8 oz) plain (all-purpose) flour

2 teaspoons baking powder

60 g (2¼ oz) desiccated coconut

50 g (1¾ oz) quick oats

½ teaspoon ground cinnamon

⅛ teaspoon fine sea salt

160 g (5½ oz) Plum & Star Anise Jam (page 207), or good red jam

VANILLA BUTTERCREAM

100 g (3½ oz) unsalted butter, softened

200 g (7 oz) icing (confectioners') sugar mixture

1 teaspoon vanilla bean paste

1 tablespoon full-cream (whole) milk

Place the butter, sugar, vanilla and golden syrup in the bowl of a stand mixer with a paddle attachment and beat until light and fluffy. Scrape down the side of the bowl, then add the egg and beat well to combine.

In a separate mixing bowl, mix together the flour, baking powder, coconut, oats, cinnamon and salt. Add the dry ingredients to the creamed butter mixture, mixing briefly to form a soft dough. Set the dough aside, in the bowl, for 15–30 minutes somewhere cool (in the fridge if the weather is hot) to firm up a little before shaping.

While the dough is resting, preheat the oven to 150°C (300°F) fan-forced and line three baking trays with baking paper.

When the dough has rested, use your hands to roll heaped teaspoonfuls of dough into balls. Place on the trays, leaving a little space between the biscuits as they will spread while cooking. Flatten slightly with your fingers, or the back of a fork. Bake in the preheated oven for 15–20 minutes or until the biscuits are golden brown and smell deliciously toasty. Allow the biscuits to cool on the trays for 10 minutes before transferring to a wire rack to cool completely before filling.

While the biscuits are cooling, make the buttercream filling by placing all the ingredients in the bowl of a stand mixer with a paddle attachment and beating until light and fluffy. Sandwich the biscuits together with a generous teaspoon of buttercream and a small spoonful of jam. Allow the filling to firm before serving – or eat straight away, buttercream and jam squidging gleefully out the sides!

Flaky golden crumbs, smooth custard and puddles
of tart baked fruit; these are the pastries and tarts
that pepper my dreams.

The little bakes that are made with care and attention
when we are gifted the luxury of slow days to bake.
Delicate lemon curd and dark chocolate cream.
Tiny jam tarts and parcels of warm, fruit-filled bliss.

Some days call for speedy satisfaction, to be sure;
but others allow for longer, unhurried parcels of time
in the kitchen. This chapter is for the latter kind of
days, when the making is as therapeutic as the eating.

Rose Petals, Custard & Pastry-flecked Dreams

This is the pastry I use for all my sweet tart shells. My kids love it so much they will eat the cooked pastry unfilled (the ultimate compliment).

Some of my recipes call for only half a batch of sweet pastry. When this is the case, freeze the other half, well-wrapped for a rainy day. Trust me, your later-self will thank you – it is akin to freezer-gold! I do so love to have a batch or two of pastry ready and waiting in the freezer. It feels like such a treat to know that in the case of a tart-emergency, one is never too far away! Simply thaw it in the fridge overnight and proceed as instructed in the recipe.

Short Sweet Pastry

MAKES APPROXIMATELY 650 g (1 lb 7 oz) PASTRY

200 g (7 oz) unsalted butter, softened
40 g (1½ oz) icing (confectioners') sugar mixture
1 teaspoon vanilla bean paste
1 egg, lightly beaten
350 g (12 oz) plain (all-purpose) flour
¼ teaspoon fine sea salt

Place the softened butter in the bowl of a stand mixer with a paddle attachment and mix on low speed until smooth. Add the sugar and vanilla and mix again until well combined. You're not looking for a light and fluffy texture here, just a uniformly creamy consistency. Add the egg and continue to beat, now on medium speed until the mixture comes together, scraping down the side of the bowl once or twice. It can take a few minutes for the egg to incorporate, especially if your kitchen is cold, so just take your time here.

Add the flour and salt to the bowl and mix on low speed until the pastry just comes together. Tip the whole lot out onto a clean work surface and gently bring the pastry and any loose flour together with your hands. Squish and knead ever so slightly until smooth, then divide the pastry in two. Roll each portion into a little fat log. Wrap well and place in the fridge to chill for an hour or two (or up to 2 days), or until the pastry is firm enough to work with.

If your pastry has been in the fridge for longer than a couple of hours, leave it out at room temperature for 30–60 minutes before using as directed in the recipe.

I often make this pastry in the evening, when the house is quiet, and everyone else has gone to bed. I like that I can make it with my hands – no noisy mixer required. There is something thoroughly therapeutic about the repetitive motion of 'stretching' the butter into the flour. Also therapeutic is going to bed, safe in the knowledge that a batch of something delicious is in the offing!

This is my go-to pastry for galettes and fruit turnovers. It's lovely and flaky and works for all manner of bakes. Spelt flour gives it a subtle, sweet nutty flavour and the sour cream keeps it delightfully tender. Thank you to Danielle Alvarez for showing me how to incorporate butter in little sheets into pastry in this manner – it makes for such a beautifully light, flaky crust.

Flaky Sour Cream Spelt Pastry

MAKES APPROXIMATELY 650 g (1 lb 7 oz) PASTRY

300 g (10½ oz) white spelt flour
2 teaspoons caster (superfine) sugar
¼ teaspoon fine sea salt
200 g (7 oz) unsalted butter, cold, cubed
175 g (5½ oz) sour cream

Place the flour, sugar and salt in a mixing bowl and mix together briefly. Scatter in the cold, cubed butter and use your fingertips to coat all the pieces in flour. Working piece by piece, squash and stretch each piece of butter between your thumb and forefinger – you're aiming for thin sheets of butter, rather than pebbles here.

When all the butter has been squashed, toss it through the flour again and add the sour cream. Use your hands to work the sour cream into the flour and butter mixture. As soon as the pastry starts to come together, tip the whole lot out onto a clean work surface and gently bring it together with your hands. Knead briefly, just to catch all the dry bits. The pastry may seem a little dry and shaggy at this point, but that's fine – this makes for a lighter, flakier result, and it will hydrate as it rests.

Shape the pastry into a rough rectangle, then fold it in half. Press the pastry back out into a rectangle shape and fold it over on itself one more time. Wrap well and place in the fridge to rest for a couple of hours, or overnight. If leaving for longer than 2 hours in the fridge, stand at room temperature for half an hour before rolling out and using as directed.

Sweet, soft baked peaches, short, crisp pastry and silky-smooth custard cream. Need I say more? These little peach-crowned custard tarts are a true joy to eat!

Now, I'm just going to put it out there – this is not a quick recipe, but nor does that mean it is difficult. I think sometimes 'simple' has become synonymous with 'quick', but really, they are two very different things. There are a few different components required to put these tarts together, but I promise you that none of them are difficult. A little planning helps here too, as the pastry, baked peaches and custard cream can all be made ahead of time. And then you can serve them to friends with the smug satisfaction of someone who has just made pastry and custard from scratch. Oh, yes!

Peach & Custard Cream Tarts

MAKES 10 SMALL TARTS

½ quantity Short Sweet Pastry (page 76), rested

A little plain (all-purpose) flour, to dust

½ quantity baked peaches (see page 212)

Unsprayed edible rose petals, to decorate (optional)

CUSTARD CREAM

200 ml (7 fl oz) full-cream (whole) milk

2 teaspoons vanilla bean paste

2 egg yolks

55 g (2 oz) caster (superfine) sugar

2 tablespoons (20 g/¾ oz) cornflour (cornstarch)

Pinch of fine sea salt

40 g (1½ oz) unsalted butter, cubed

100 ml (3½ fl oz) thickened (whipping) cream

First, make the custard for the custard cream by heating the milk and vanilla in a small saucepan over low heat. Heat the milk to just below a simmer, then remove from the heat.

While the milk is warming, place the egg yolks in a mixing bowl. Add the sugar and use a hand whisk to thoroughly combine. Add the cornflour and salt to the bowl and continue to whisk until the mixture becomes thick and smooth, and paler in colour.

Trickle the hot milk into the egg yolk mixture, whisking constantly. When combined, return the mixture to the saucepan and place over medium–low heat. Cook, stirring continually with a whisk until the custard thickens and begins to bubble. Cook for a further minute, whisking quite fast, to cook out the cornflour, then remove the pan from the heat.

Strain the custard into a bowl through a fine sieve and stir in the butter, 1 tablespoon at a time, mixing until smooth. Cover the surface directly with plastic wrap and refrigerate until cold, 2–3 hours, or overnight.

Next, prepare the tart shells. Preheat the oven to 170°C (325°F) fan-forced and place ten loose-bottomed tart (flan) tins with a base measurement of 6 cm (2½ inches), 2 cm (¾ inch) deep, on a baking tray.

Cut your rested pastry log into 10 equal rounds. Working with one piece at a time, scrunch each round in your hand once or twice to make the pastry malleable, then roll it into a ball. →

Place the balls on a lightly floured surface and, using a rolling pin, roll each ball out to a 10–12 cm (4–4½ inch) circle. Gently ease the rolled pastry into the tins, pressing the pastry snugly into the base and sides. If the pastry has warmed up a lot, refrigerate the tart shells for 30 minutes before baking.

Trim off any excess pastry using a small sharp knife and place a square of baking paper or foil into each pastry shell. Fill with baking beads and bake in the preheated oven for 25 minutes, until deeply golden all over. Remove from the oven and allow the tart shells to cool with the baking beads in them. (This step can be done the day before you want to serve the tarts – just store the cooled, cooked tart shells in an airtight container until ready to bake.)

When ready to assemble the tarts, finish the custard cream by whisking the thickened cream to soft peaks. Place the chilled custard in the bowl of a stand mixer with a whisk attachment and whisk briefly until smooth. Add the softly whipped cream and continue to mix until smooth and thick. Try not to overmix here or the custard may end up too runny.

To serve, top the cooked tart shells with a generous tablespoon of custard cream, followed by a baked peach half. Decorate with rose petals (if using) and serve with smug satisfaction!

STORE & SHARE *These little tarts are best eaten within a couple of hours of assembling. The pastry cream will keep happily for 2–3 days (well covered) in a container in the fridge, as will the baked peaches. The cooked pastry shells will keep for a couple of days in an airtight container at room temperature. For a breezy dessert or afternoon tea, prepare all the elements the day before you want to serve the tarts.*

I love a good galette. I mean, who doesn't? Jammy fruit and crisp, flaky pastry are always a good idea, I think. Even better when they are little, hand-sized tarts, meaning the ratio of pastry to fruit is on point, and you don't even have to share!

When we bought our house in the Blue Mountains we were lucky enough to inherit a veggie patch with a few crowns of rhubarb in it. Happily, they are still going strong, and when we have exhausted our small supply, I know I can always rely on my parents for a beautiful bunch. Dad seems to have finally cracked the secret to growing the longest-stemmed, most gloriously crimson rhubarb I have ever seen! I am delighted and jealous in equal measure.

Rhubarb & Strawberry Galettes

MAKES 10 HAND-SIZED GALETTES

Plain (all-purpose) flour, to dust

1 quantity Flaky Sour Cream Spelt Pastry (page 77), rested

1 egg, well beaten, to glaze

2 tablespoons caster (superfine) sugar, for sprinkling

2 tablespoons Strawberry & Rhubarb Jam (page 211), or store-bought strawberry jam

Thick (double) cream or ice cream, to serve (optional)

FRUIT FILLING

300 g (10½ oz) rhubarb, cut into 5 cm (2 inch) pieces, stems halved or quartered

250 g (9 oz) strawberries, hulled and quartered

80 g (2¾ oz) caster (superfine) sugar

Juice of ½ lemon

1 teaspoon vanilla bean paste

1 tablespoon (10 g/¼ oz) cornflour (cornstarch)

First, make the fruit filling by placing the chopped rhubarb, strawberries, sugar, lemon juice, vanilla and cornflour in a mixing bowl, tossing to combine. Make sure the cornflour and sugar are well mixed in, then set the mixture aside while you roll out your pastry.

Preheat the oven to 180°C (350°F) fan-forced and place two baking trays in the oven to heat up. Cut two sheets of baking paper the same size as your baking trays and set aside.

Next, lightly dust your work surface with flour then, using a rolling pin, roll the rested pastry out into a large rectangle, roughly 30 x 60 cm (12 x 24 inches), 3–4 mm (⅛–³⁄₁₆ inch) thick. Cut out eight 14 cm (5½ inch) pastry rounds and set aside. Gather up the left-over pastry, dust with a little flour and roll it out again, cutting out two more rounds. This pastry doesn't like to be rolled out too many times, so try and handle it as little as possible. (If the pastry has become very soft, return the rounds to the fridge for half an hour before assembling the galettes.)

Place five pastry rounds on each sheet of prepared baking paper. Divide the fruit filling between the rounds, discarding any excess liquid left in the bottom of the bowl. Pile the fruit into a little mound in the centre of the pastry, leaving a 2.5 cm (1 inch) border of clean pastry. Then, working with one galette at a time, carefully fold the pastry border over to enclose the edges of the fruit, pleating and pinching it in place with your fingers. Repeat with the remaining galettes. Brush the pastry borders with beaten egg and sprinkle the galettes liberally with the 2 tablespoons of caster sugar, making sure to cover the pastry. →

Carefully remove the preheated baking trays from the oven and gently slide the galettes on their baking paper onto the trays. Return to the oven for 25–35 minutes, or until the pastry on the galettes is dark golden, the bottoms are crisp and the fruit juices are starting to bubble and caramelise.

When the galettes are cooked, heat the strawberry and rhubarb jam with 1 teaspoon of water, until bubbling (I do this in a small bowl in the microwave). Brush the hot jam over the surface of the fruit on the galettes. Allow the galettes to cool on the trays for 15 minutes or so before serving warm or at room temperature, with cream or ice cream if you like.

STORE & SHARE *The galettes are best shared and eaten on the day they are made (warm from the oven if at all possible!) but will keep in an airtight container in the fridge for a day or so – just reheat gently before serving.*

I'm not sure that I ever ate these as a child and yet jam tarts still feel impossibly nostalgic. Maybe it's the association with Alice in Wonderland, or maybe it is simply being allowed to essentially eat jam by the spoonful, that makes these so wonderful? Either way, they spark a childlike joy in me, so I'm keeping them! The look on my kids' faces when they come home from school to a plate of these is also rather magic. The only rule here is to use good jam, because it really is the star.

Jam Tarts

MAKES 24 BITE-SIZED TARTS

1 quantity Short Sweet Pastry (page 76), rested

A little plain (all-purpose) flour, to dust

160 g (5½ oz) Strawberry & Rhubarb Jam (page 211), or other good jam

160 g (5½ oz) Roast Apricot Jam (page 206), or other good jam

160 g (5½ oz) Plum & Star Anise Jam (page 207), or other good jam

1 egg, well beaten, to glaze

Caster (superfine) sugar, to sprinkle

Thick (double) cream, to serve (optional)

Preheat the oven to 180°C (350°F) fan-forced and get two 12-hole patty pan tins out ready (these are the small shallow, rounded tins for old-fashioned patty cakes). You can do the tarts in two batches if you only have one tin.

Prepare the pastry for the tart shells by cutting the rested pastry logs into four or five pieces each. Working with one piece at a time, use the heel of your hand to stretch and smear the pastry out over a clean work surface, to make the pastry malleable. Bundle all the pastry back into one piece and knead very briefly. Shape into a rough rectangle. Place on a lightly floured surface and, using a rolling pin, roll the pastry out until it is about 2–3 mm (¹⁄₁₆–⅛ inch) thick.

Use a round or fluted cutter that is slightly bigger than your patty pan holes (about 7 cm/2¾ inches) to cut out as many rounds from your pastry sheet as you can. Re-roll the pastry and cut out the remaining rounds, along with some small flower or heart shapes (use cutters or cut them freehand) to place on top of the tarts, if you like. Place one pastry round in the base of each patty pan hole, gently pressing it into place. If the pastry has warmed up a lot, refrigerate the tart shells and toppers for 30 minutes before baking.

Fill each pastry shell with about 2 teaspoons of one of the jams, alternating flavours, and making sure to remove any star anise pieces from the plum jam. Try not to overfill the tarts or they will bubble over while cooking. →

Gently place a pastry flower or heart on top, if using. Brush the toppers with the egg wash and sprinkle with a little caster sugar. Bake in the preheated oven for 12–18 minutes, or until the pastry is golden and the jam is bubbling.

Allow the tarts to cool in the tins for a couple of minutes before carefully removing them using a flat-bladed knife and placing them on a wire rack to cool (you want to take the tarts out before any sugar or jam-spills cool and cement them to the tin, but be gentle as the pastry will still be soft). Allow to cool to room temperature before serving – with a spoonful of thick cream if you like!

STORE & SHARE *These little tarts are best eaten on the day they are baked. So share them with some dear folk and a big pot of tea – while pondering what an excellent invention jam is!*

Chocolate and hazelnut, a well-loved classic for good reason. When I was testing recipes for this book, I spent a busy couple of weeks staying at my parents' house – filling their table (and their neighbours') with sweet baked goods. They looked after the kids, I fed everyone too much sugar, and the oven was never turned off! When we left, I squirrelled away two of these little beauties at the back of the fridge for Dad. Mum promptly found them and generously gifted them to a friend who had dropped in for tea! Dad was devastated. At which stage I knew I could stop testing them – they could go in the book! Sorry Dad, maybe Mum will make you a batch now ...?

Chocolate Hazelnut Tarts

MAKES 10 SMALL TARTS

½ quantity Short Sweet Pastry (page 76), rested

A little plain (all-purpose) flour, to dust

60 g (2¼ oz) hazelnuts

Thick (double) cream, to serve (optional)

CHOCOLATE FILLING

125 ml (4 fl oz) pure (single) cream

1 teaspoon vanilla bean paste

180 g (6½ oz) dark chocolate (45–55% cocoa solids), roughly chopped

2 tablespoons caster (superfine) sugar

100 g (3½ oz) sour cream

1 egg, lightly beaten

Pinch of fine sea salt

Preheat the oven to 170°C (325°F) fan-forced and place ten loose-bottomed tart (flan) tins with a base measurement of 6 cm (2½ inches), 2 cm (¾ inch) deep, on a baking tray.

First, prepare the tart shells by cutting your rested pastry log into 10 equal rounds. Working with one piece at a time, scrunch each round in your hand once or twice to make the pastry malleable, then roll into a ball. Place on a lightly floured work surface and, using a rolling pin, roll each ball out to a 10–12 cm (4–4½ inch) circle (about 3 mm/⅛ inch thick). Gently ease the rolled pastry rounds into the tins, pressing the pastry snugly into the base and up the side of each tin. If the pastry has warmed up a lot, refrigerate the tart shells for 30 minutes before baking.

Use a small sharp knife to trim off any excess pastry from around the rim of the tarts, then place a square of baking paper or foil into each pastry shell. Fill with baking beads and place in the oven to bake for 20–25 minutes, until golden all over. Remove from the oven and allow the tart shells to cool with the baking beads in them. (This step can be done the day before you want to serve the tarts – just store the cooked cooled tart shells in an airtight container.)

Lower the oven temperature to 130°C (250°F). Place the hazelnuts on a small baking tray and bake for 5–8 minutes, or until they are fragrant, and the skins will slip off the nuts. Place the nuts in a clean tea towel (dish towel) and rub together to remove most of the skins – it doesn't really matter if a bit of the skin stays on. Set aside. →

While the tart shells and nuts are cooling, make the chocolate filling by heating the cream and vanilla in a small saucepan until just below a simmer. Remove from the heat and add the chocolate to the pan. Allow the mixture to sit for a minute or two to melt the chocolate before using a small whisk to mix until smooth. Mix in the sugar, followed by the sour cream, then the egg and salt, whisking until smooth.

When the tart shells are cool, remove the baking paper and baking beads. Divide the chocolate filling evenly among the tarts, and top with the roasted hazelnuts. Bake in the oven for 12–18 minutes or until the surface of the chocolate filling is set, but is still a little wobbly in the centre. The filling will continue to cook as it cools.

Allow the tarts to cool in their tins before carefully turning them out and serving with a spoonful of cream, if you like.

STORE & SHARE *While best eaten on the day they are made, these little tarts will keep happily in an airtight container in the fridge for 2–3 days – just return to room temperature before serving. Share with good friends only, and don't forget to save one for your dad!*

These fruity delights make an excellent morning or afternoon tea – although to be honest I also often eat them for breakfast the morning after I've baked them, and that is truly heaven in a fruity, pastry-encased form. I figure they cover a few of the breakfast essentials: fruit and carbohydrate; and if I add cream, then I can tick dairy off my list too. Win, win! Make the spelt pastry the day before you want to bake these for an even simpler time of it.

Apricot Turnovers

MAKES 10 TURNOVERS

A little plain (all-purpose) flour,
  to dust
1 quantity Flaky Sour Cream
  Spelt Pastry (page 77), rested
1 egg, well beaten, to glaze
Thick (double) cream or ice
  cream, to serve (optional)

FRUIT FILLING
600 g (1 lb 5 oz) ripe apricots
110 g (3¾ oz) caster (superfine)
  sugar, plus extra to sprinkle
2 teaspoons vanilla bean paste
2 teaspoons lemon juice
2 tablespoons (20 g/¾ oz)
  cornflour (cornstarch)
½ teaspoon ground cardamom
A pinch of fine sea salt

Preheat the oven to 180°C (350°F) fan-forced and place two baking trays in the oven to heat up. Cut two sheets of baking paper the same size as your baking trays and set aside.

First, prepare the pastry. Lightly dust a work surface with a little flour, then, using a rolling pin, roll out the rested pastry into a large rectangle roughly 30 x 60 cm (12 x 24 inches), 3–4 mm (⅛–³⁄₁₆ inch) thick. Cut out eight 14 cm (5½ inch) rounds of pastry and set aside. Gather up the left-over pastry, dust with a little flour and roll it out again, cutting two more rounds. This pastry doesn't like to be rolled out too many times, so try and handle it as little as possible. (If the pastry has become very soft, return the rounds to the fridge for half an hour before assembling the turnovers.)

Wash the apricots and cut them in half, discarding the pits. Chop the apricots into 2 cm (¾ inch) pieces and place in a mixing bowl along with the sugar, vanilla, lemon juice, cornflour, cardamom and salt. Toss well, making sure the cornflour and sugar are well mixed in.

Place the pastry rounds on the prepared baking paper (five per sheet) and brush around the edges of the pastry with some of the beaten egg. Divide the apricot mixture evenly between the pastry rounds, piling it in little mounds in the centre, and discard any excess liquid at the bottom of the bowl. →

Working with one turnover at a time, carefully bring one side of the pastry over to meet the other, stretching a little if necessary to enclose the fruit filling. (Don't worry if you get a few little tears in the pastry here, it won't matter at all. Just pinch the pastry together to patch up any large holes.) Press the seam together, then use your fingers to pleat the pastry, or simply press firmly together with the back of a fork. Repeat with the remaining turnovers.

Brush the tops of the turnovers with the remaining beaten egg to glaze and sprinkle liberally with the extra caster sugar. Use a small sharp knife to cut a little vent in the top of each turnover. Carefully remove the preheated baking trays from the oven and slide the turnovers on their baking paper onto the trays. Return to the oven for 25–35 minutes, or until the turnovers are golden brown and the apricot juices are starting to bubble and caramelise. Allow to cool on the trays for 15 minutes or so before serving warm or at room temperature. Cream or ice cream is a really good idea here.

STORE & SHARE *The turnovers are best eaten on the day they are made (warm from the oven if at all possible!) but will keep in an airtight container in the fridge for a day or two – just reheat gently in the oven before serving.*

These sun-shiny little lovelies truly are heaven in a tiny tart shell! And the perfect foil for a gloomy afternoon. I umm'd and ahh'd about whether or not to include a torched meringue top on these teeny tarts, but decided (much to my kids' disgust), that I preferred them naked – their mouth-puckering citrus flavour unadulterated.

Do take the time to rub the lemon thyme and zest thoroughly through the sugar at the start of the recipe – this not only ensures a beautifully fragrant, lightly herbaceous lemon filling, but is also wildly therapeutic! Use the left-over egg whites for a batch of Lemon & Fennel Seed Amaretti (page 180), or Baby Meringues (page 52) which, incidentally, also work beautifully as an accompaniment to the tarts – meringues after all! My kids will be relieved!

Lemon Gems

MAKES 10 LITTLE TARTS

½ quantity Short Sweet Pastry (page 76), rested

A little plain (all-purpose) flour, to dust

Thick (double) cream, to serve (optional)

LEMON FILLING

110 g (3¾ oz) caster (superfine) sugar

Finely grated zest of 1 lemon

2 teaspoons lemon thyme leaves

1 egg, plus 3 yolks

2 teaspoons plain (all-purpose) flour

Pinch of fine sea salt

125 ml (4 fl oz) lemon juice (from 3–4 lemons)

125 ml (4 fl oz) pure (single) cream

First, make the lemon filling by placing the sugar, lemon zest and lemon thyme leaves in a mixing bowl. Use your fingers to rub the zest and thyme through the sugar until the mixture is fragrant and resembles damp sand. Add the whole egg and egg yolks to the bowl and use a hand whisk to mix for a minute or so until well combined. Whisk in the flour and salt before adding the lemon juice and cream, whisking again until smooth. Cover and place in the fridge to infuse for at least an hour, or overnight, while you bake the tart shells.

When ready to make the tarts, preheat the oven to 170°C (325°F) fan-forced and place ten loose-bottomed tart (flan) tins with a base measurement of 6 cm (2½ inches), 2 cm (¾ inch) deep (or equivalent-sized tins) on a baking tray.

Prepare the tart shells by cutting your rested pastry log into 10 equal rounds. Working with one piece at a time, scrunch each round in your hand once or twice to make the pastry malleable, then roll into a ball. Place on a lightly floured surface and, using a rolling pin, roll each ball out to a 10–12 cm (4–4½ inch) circle. Gently ease the rolled pastry into the tins, pressing the pastry snugly into the base and up the sides of each tin. If the pastry has warmed up a lot, refrigerate the tart shells for 30 minutes before baking.

Use a small sharp knife to trim off any excess pastry, then place a square of baking paper or foil into each pastry shell. Fill with baking beads and bake in the preheated oven for 20–25 minutes, or until deeply golden all over. →

Remove from the oven and allow the tart shells to cool with the baking beads in them. (This step can be done the day before you want to serve the tarts; just store the cooled, cooked tart shells in an airtight container until ready to bake.)

Lower the oven temperature to 120°C (250°F). While the pastry shells are cooling, take the lemon filling out of the fridge. Strain the mixture through a fine sieve into a jug that pours well, then use a piece of paper towel to skim off as much foam from the surface as you can.

When the tart shells are cool, remove the baking paper and baking beads. Gently pour the lemon filling into the pastry cases. I do this while the tray is in the oven as I find it easier than juggling the tart shells back to the oven filled with the runny lemon filling. Bake the tarts for 15–20 minutes, or until the filling is just set, but still a little wobbly in the middle. The curd will continue to cook as it cools.

Allow the tarts to cool to room temperature before serving, with a dollop of thick cream , if you like.

STORE & SHARE *These little tarts are at their best on the day they are baked, but will store in an airtight container in the fridge overnight. The pastry will soften a little, and the curd may crack the longer they are stored, but they will still taste delicious!*

These little tarts are one of my all-time favourites. Combining fragrant ground tea, nutty pistachio frangipane, and a halo of sunshiny baked apricot, they really are delicious! Please don't be put off by the number of steps in the recipe – it takes a little time and forethought, to be sure, but none of it is difficult, truly, I promise. And the end result is very, very rewarding (not to mention tasty!).

Little Apricot & Earl Grey Tarts

½ quantity Short Sweet Pastry (page 76), rested

A little plain (all-purpose) flour, to dust

5 ripe apricots, halved, pits removed

2 tablespoons Roast Apricot Jam (page 206), or good apricot jam

2 tablespoons chopped pistachio kernels, to serve

Thick (double) cream, to serve (optional)

FRANGIPANE

80 g (2¾ oz) pistachio kernels

1 teaspoon loose-leaf Earl Grey tea

60 g (2¼ oz) unsalted butter, very soft

55 g (2 oz) caster (superfine) sugar

½ teaspoon vanilla bean paste

1 egg, lightly beaten

1½ tablespoons plain (all-purpose) flour

Pinch of fine sea salt

Preheat the oven to 170°C (325°F) fan-forced and place ten loose-bottomed tart (flan) tins with a base measurement of 6 cm (2½ inches), 2 cm (¾ inch) deep, on a baking tray.

Place the 80 g (2¾ oz) of pistachio kernels and the Earl Grey tea in a small blender or food processor and grind until fine. Set aside.

Prepare the tart shells by cutting your rested pastry log into 10 equal rounds. Working with one piece at a time, scrunch each round in your hand once or twice to make the pastry malleable, then roll into a ball. Place on a lightly floured work surface and, using a rolling pin, roll each ball out to a 10–12 cm (4–4½ inch) round (about 3 mm/⅛ inch thick). Gently ease the rolled pastry into the tins, pressing the pastry snugly into the base and up the sides of each tin. If the pastry has warmed up a lot, refrigerate the tart shells for 30 minutes before baking.

Use a small sharp knife to trim off any excess pastry, then place a square of baking paper or foil into each pastry shell. Fill with baking beads and bake in the preheated oven for 20–25 minutes, until deeply golden all over. Remove from the oven and allow the tart shells to cool with the baking beads in them. (This step can be done the day before you want to serve the tarts; just store the cooled, cooked tart shells in an airtight container until ready to bake.) →

While the tart shells are cooling, make the pistachio frangipane by placing the softened butter, sugar, vanilla, egg and ground pistachio tea mixture in a mixing bowl and beating until light (you can do this by hand with a wooden spoon, just make sure the butter is really soft before you begin). Add the flour and salt and stir gently to combine. Set aside.

When the tart shells are cool, remove the baking beads and baking paper. Spoon a tablespoon of frangipane into each shell, smoothing gently with the back of a spoon. Nestle an apricot half, cut side up, into each tart. Lower the oven temperature to 160°C (325°F) fan-forced and return the tarts to the oven for 20–25 minutes or until the frangipane is golden and cooked through and the apricots start to bubble.

Heat the apricot jam with 1 teaspoon of water, until bubbling (I do this in a small bowl in the microwave). Brush the cooked tarts with hot jam and sprinkle with the extra chopped pistachios. Allow the tarts to cool in their tins before carefully turning them out and serving – with a dollop of thick (double) cream if you like!

STORE & SHARE *Best eaten on the day they are made, these little tarts are excellent shared for afternoon tea. Any leftovers will keep happily in an airtight container in the fridge for 2–3 days – just return to room temperature before serving.*

I think custard tarts will always remind me of my little brother who, as a child, had a particular penchant for the country-bakery-variety. My dad was rather fond of them too, come to think of it. And my big brother wouldn't ever turn one down either. Must run on the male side of the family ...!

I have to say though, that while I was never particularly enamoured by the bakery custard tart, even I am rather fond of this variety. Silky smooth sour cream custard, hiding a gem of tart baked fruit or boozy soaked prune, all housed in flaky spelt pastry. Could be worse. Could definitely be worse! Make the pastry and baked fruit the day before you want to bake these little tarts for an excellently fuss-free time.

Baked Custard & Plum Tarts

MAKES 12 TARTS

A little plain (all-purpose) flour, to dust

1 quantity Flaky Sour Cream Spelt Pastry (page 77), rested

1 quantity baked plums (see page 212), or Pedro Ximénez–steeped prunes (see note on page 105)

Ground cinnamon or nutmeg, to dust (optional)

CUSTARD FILLING

250 g (9 oz) sour cream

250 ml (9 fl oz) pure (single) cream

4 eggs

140 g (5 oz) caster (superfine) sugar

2 teaspoons vanilla bean paste

Place twelve loose-bottomed tart (flan) tins with a base measurement of 8 cm (3¼ inches), 3 cm (1¼ inches) deep, on two large baking trays.

Lightly dust a work surface with flour then, using a rolling pin, roll the rested pastry out into a large rectangle, roughly 3 mm (⅛ inch) thick. Cut out 12 rounds of pastry, slightly bigger than your tart tins (about 14 cm/5½ inches in diameter), gathering up the offcuts and re-rolling the pastry as required. This pastry doesn't like to be rolled out too many times, so try and handle it as little as possible.

Gently ease the pastry rounds into the tart tins, pressing the pastry snugly into the base and up the side of each tin. Refrigerate the tart shells for 30 minutes before using a small sharp knife to trim off any excess pastry around the rims.

While the tart shells are chilling, preheat the oven to 170°C (325°F) fan-forced.

When the pastry has chilled, place a square of baking paper or foil into each pastry shell, and fill with baking beads. Place the tarts back on the baking trays and bake in the preheated oven for 30 minutes. Remove the beads and baking paper or foil, and place the tart shells back in the oven for a further 5–8 minutes, or until the pastry is golden all over. Remove from the oven and allow the tart shells to cool slightly.

Lower the oven temperature to 130°C (250°F). While the tart shells are cooling, make the custard filling by combining the sour cream, pure cream, eggs, sugar and vanilla in a mixing bowl. Whisk well to combine, then strain the mixture through a fine sieve into a jug. →

When the tart shells have cooled, place a baked plum half (or 2–3 steeped prunes) in the base of each tart shell, gently squashing the fruit to cover the base of the tart. Carefully pour in the strained custard mixture, being careful not to overfill the tarts. I do this while the tray is in the oven as I find it easier than juggling it back to the oven filled with the runny custard filling. Dust the custard lightly with ground cinnamon or freshly grated nutmeg (if using).

Bake the tarts for a further 25–35 minutes, or until the surface of the custard is just set, but the centre is still a little wobbly when jiggled. The custard will continue to cook as it cools. Allow the tarts to cool to room temperature before eating them straight away, or placing them in the fridge to chill until ready to serve.

PEDRO XIMÉNEZ–STEEPED PRUNES To make Pedro Ximénez–steeped prunes (boozy and delicious!), place 250 g (9 oz) pitted prunes in a small saucepan along with 125 ml (4 fl oz) Pedro Ximénez sherry. Simmer over low heat for 3–5 minutes, stirring once or twice, until the prunes are starting to soften. Remove from the heat and allow to cool in the pan with the lid on.

STORE & SHARE *While I like to eat these custard tarts at room temperature on the day they are made, they also keep well in the fridge for a day or two. They can be made the day before you want to serve them, and will wait patiently in the fridge until you are ready to eat them!*

December is a funny time of year, isn't it? The want for festivities and cheer is high, but end-of-year fatigue is also very real. I do find, however, that a spot of Christmas baking usually does the trick – tipping the pendulum firmly in favour of cheerfulness (and maybe overindulgence).

Fruit mince pies are one of the mandatory items on my Christmas bake list – my mum always makes them in the days leading up to Christmas and it is a tradition I also have adopted. Homemade fruit mince really does make these little pies special, but if you're pressed for time, a good quality store-bought one will work too. I like my pies with a layer of frangipane between the pastry and fruit, and maybe with a spoonful of thick (double) cream. Delicious!

Fruit Mince & Frangipane Pies

MAKES 24 BITE-SIZED PIES

1 quantity Short Sweet Pastry (page 76), rested

A little plain (all-purpose) flour, to dust

450 g (1 lb) Good Fruit Mince (page 217), or use quality store-bought

1 egg, well beaten, to glaze

Raw (demerara) sugar, to sprinkle

Thick (double) cream, to serve (optional)

FRANGIPANE

60 g (2¼ oz) unsalted butter, very soft

55 g (2 oz) caster (superfine) sugar

½ teaspoon vanilla bean paste

1 egg, lightly beaten

80 g (2¾ oz) almond meal

1 tablespoon plain (all-purpose) flour

Pinch of fine sea salt

Preheat the oven to 180°C (350°F) fan-forced and get two 12-hole patty pan tins out ready (these are the small shallow, rounded tins for old-fashioned patty cakes). You can do the tarts in two batches if you only have one tin.

First, make the frangipane by placing the soft butter, sugar, vanilla, egg and almond meal in a mixing bowl and beating until light (you can do this by hand with a wooden spoon, just make sure the butter is really soft before you begin). Add the flour and salt and stir gently to combine. Set aside.

Next, prepare the pastry for the pies by cutting the rested pastry logs into five or six pieces each. Working with one piece at a time, use the heel of your hand to stretch and smear the pastry out over a clean work surface, to make the pastry malleable. Bundle all the pastry back into one piece and knead very briefly. Shape into a rough rectangle. Place on a lightly floured surface and, using a rolling pin, roll the pastry out until it is about 2–3 mm (1⁄16–1⁄8 inch) thick.

Use a round cutter that is slightly bigger than your patty pan holes (about 7 cm/2¾ inches) to cut out as many rounds from the rolled pastry as you can. Re-roll the pastry and cut out the remaining rounds, along with 24 star shapes (I use 4–5 cm/1½–2 inch star cutters) to place on top of the pies. Place one pastry round into the base of each patty pan hole, gently pressing it into place. If the pastry has warmed up a lot, refrigerate the tart shells and stars for 30 minutes before baking. →

Fill each pastry shell with a teaspoon of frangipane and top with 2 teaspoons of fruit mince. Gently place a star on top of each pie, brush with the beaten egg and sprinkle with a little raw sugar.

Bake in the preheated oven for 15–18 minutes, or until the pastry is golden and the fruit mince is bubbling. Allow the pies to cool in the tins for a couple of minutes before carefully removing them using a flat-bladed knife and placing on a wire rack to cool (you want to take the pies out before any sugar or fruit mince spills cool and cement them to the tin, but be gentle as the pastry will still be soft!).

STORE & SHARE *Mince pies are best eaten the day they are baked, but will keep quite happily in an airtight container at room temperature for 2 or 3 days (ours never last that long!). Serve with a spoonful of thick cream if you are so inclined. Mince pies also make a wonderful addition to an edible Christmas hamper, along with some gingerbread (page 201) and a jar of homemade jam or sunny passionfruit curd (pages 206–11).*

These are really wonderful with a big pot of tea on a cold wintery day. Crisp, flaky, spelt pastry plays host to a slick of nutty hazelnut frangipane, soft Pedro Ximénez–soaked prunes and a fan of baked pear. Top with a dollop of thick (double) cream. Winter comfort in tart-form.

Pear, Prune & Hazelnut Galettes

MAKES 10 HAND-SIZED GALETTES

300 g (10½ oz) pitted prunes

125 ml (4 fl oz) Pedro Ximénez

A little plain (all-purpose) flour, to dust

1 quantity Flaky Sour Cream Spelt Pastry (page 77), rested

5 small beurre bosc pears

1 egg, well beaten, to glaze

2 tablespoons raw (demerara) sugar, to sprinkle

Thick (double) cream, to serve (optional)

HAZELNUT FRANGIPANE

100 g (3½ oz) hazelnuts

60 g (2¼ oz) unsalted butter, very soft

55 g (2 oz) caster (superfine) sugar

½ teaspoon vanilla bean paste

1 egg, lightly beaten

1 tablespoon spelt flour

Pinch of fine sea salt

First, place the prunes and Pedro Ximénez in a small saucepan. Cover with a lid and place the pan over medium heat. Bring the mixture to the boil, then reduce the heat and allow it to simmer with the lid askew for 3 minutes. Turn the heat off, give the prunes a stir, then place the lid back on. Set aside and allow the prunes to cool.

While the prunes are cooling, make the hazelnut frangipane. Place 75 g (2½ oz) of the hazelnuts in a small blender or spice grinder and blitz to a fine meal. Roughly chop the remaining 25 g (1 oz) of hazelnuts and stir them through the hazelnut meal. Set aside.

Place the softened butter, caster sugar and vanilla in a mixing bowl and use a wooden spoon to beat until light. Add the egg, followed by the hazelnut mixture, spelt flour and salt. Mix well until the frangipane is combined and light. Set aside.

Preheat the oven to 180°C (350°F) fan-forced and place two baking trays in the oven to heat up. Cut two sheets of baking paper the same size as your baking trays and set aside.

Next, prepare the pastry. Lightly dust a work surface with flour then, using a rolling pin, roll the rested pastry out into a large rectangle, roughly 30 x 60 cm (12 x 24 inches), 3–4 mm (⅛–³⁄₁₆ inch) thick. Cut out eight 14 cm (5½ inch) rounds of pastry and set aside. →

Gather up the left-over pastry, dust with a little flour and roll it out again, cutting out two more rounds. This pastry doesn't like to be rolled out too many times, so try and handle it as little as possible. (If the pastry has become very soft, return the rounds to the fridge for half an hour before assembling the galettes.)

Place the pastry rounds on your prepared baking paper (five per sheet). Divide the hazelnut frangipane between the pastry rounds, spreading it out into an even layer, leaving a 2.5 cm (1 inch) border clean around the edge. Divide the prunes (reserving any remaining syrup to glaze the cooked galettes) between the galettes and layer them gently on top of the frangipane. Slice the pears in half, scoop out the cores with a teaspoon and cut each into thin slices, leaving a few centimetres (about an inch) intact at the top. Fan the pears out and place one half gently on top of the prunes on each galette. Now, working with one galette at a time, carefully fold the pastry border over to enclose the edges of the fruit, pleating and pinching it in place. Repeat with the remaining galettes. Brush the pastry borders with the beaten egg and sprinkle liberally with the raw sugar.

Carefully remove the preheated baking trays from the oven and slide the galettes on their baking paper onto the trays. Return to the oven for 25–35 minutes, or until the pastry on the galettes is dark golden, the bottoms are crisp and the frangipane is cooked.

Heat the reserved prune syrup until bubbling, then gently brush it over the pear slices and prunes on the cooked galettes. Allow the galettes to cool on the trays for 15 minutes or so before serving warm or at room temperature, with thick cream, if you like.

STORE & SHARE *The galettes are best eaten on the day they are made (warm from the oven if at all possible!) but will keep in an airtight container in the fridge for a day or two – just reheat gently in the oven before serving.*

Cake: my first love and still my constant companion. Give me all the plain butter cakes and fruit-studded beauties, the chocolate cakes and ones thick with caramel and spice. Sticky, sweet and delicious, I want them all.

I've not met with many problems in life that can't be made (at least a little) better by cake. And small cakes are some of my most-loved of all; just clamouring to be eaten and shared with childlike delight. Because really, who can feel guilty about such a tiny, sweet treat?

Baby Cakes & Buttery Bliss

Some days, you just need a teeny-tiny treat – a one-bite wonder to tide you over. Other days, you need a plethora of little cakes with which to keep small hands occupied; think birthdays, picnics or rainy Sunday afternoons! These itty-bitty cakes happily satisfy all of the above, and I find the making of them as therapeutic as the eating.

Sometimes I make a double batch (that's a lot of little cakes!) and we spend a happy afternoon icing them. You can make just one flavour of Swiss meringue buttercream – or you can do as I often do and divide the icing to make three different flavours, just because I can! There is something very satisfying about a tray of beautifully iced cupcakes, not to mention the utter delight of eating the tiny, silky cloud-topped cakes. Also delightful is leaving boxes of these on the doorsteps of unsuspecting friends. Love in cake form!

Baby Cakes

MAKES 48 TINY CAKES

CAKES

125 g (4½ oz) unsalted butter, softened
125 g (4½ oz) caster (superfine) sugar
1 teaspoon vanilla bean paste
2 eggs
150 g (5½ oz) self-raising flour
Pinch of fine sea salt
80 ml (2½ fl oz) full-cream (whole) milk

SWISS MERINGUE BUTTERCREAM

3 egg whites (approximately 100 g/3½ oz)
200 g (7 oz) caster (superfine) sugar
⅛ teaspoon fine sea salt
300 g (10½ oz) unsalted butter, softened
1 teaspoon vanilla bean paste

Ingredients continued over page

Preheat the oven to 160°C (325°F) fan-forced and line four 12-hole mini muffin/cupcake tins (with 30 ml/1 fl oz capacity holes) with paper cases (or bake the cakes in batches if you have fewer tins).

For the cakes, in the bowl of a stand mixer with a paddle attachment, cream the butter, sugar and vanilla until very light and fluffy. Add the eggs, one at a time, beating well and scraping down the side of the bowl after each addition.

Add half the flour and the salt to the creamed butter mixture, stirring gently, before adding half the milk. Once incorporated, follow with the remaining flour and the remaining milk, mixing gently until just combined.

Divide the batter between the prepared cupcake cases, filling to just over half full, and bake in the preheated oven for 8–12 minutes or until the cakes are golden and cooked through. Take care not to overbake as these tiny cakes cook very quickly. Allow the cakes to cool in their trays for 10 minutes before transferring to a wire rack to cool completely.

When the cakes are cool, make the Swiss meringue buttercream by placing the egg whites, sugar and salt in a heatproof bowl set over a saucepan of gently simmering water, making sure the water doesn't touch the base of the bowl. Stir regularly with a flexible spatula until the sugar has dissolved and the egg whites are warm to the touch. →

BABY CAKES
CONTINUED

160 g (5½ oz) Strawberry &
   Rhubarb Jam (page 211), plus
   ½ teaspoon rosewater;
   or 160 g (5½ oz) Passionfruit
   Curd (page 210); or 150 g
   (5½ oz) dark chocolate
   (45–55% cocoa solids) melted
   and cooled (optional)

OPTIONAL TOPPINGS
Unsprayed edible flowers
   (dried or fresh)
Extra passionfruit curd
Chocolate shavings

Remove from the heat and place the egg white and sugar mixture in the bowl of a stand mixer with a whisk attachment. Whisk on medium-high speed for 5–8 minutes or until the meringue mixture is thick and glossy, and has cooled to room temperature.

Reduce the speed to low and whisk in the butter, a couple of tablespoons at a time. Continue to mix for a minute or so on low speed once all the butter has been incorporated, or until the mixture is glossy and smooth. When adding the butter to the meringue, there may be a point when the mixture looks like it has split or curdled – don't worry, this is quite normal and it should come back together as you continue to add the remaining butter and whisk on low speed.

Once the buttercream is smooth, add the vanilla and then either the strawberry and rhubarb jam and rosewater, the passionfruit curd, or the melted chocolate, then fold them through and mix gently, but thoroughly, until combined. Spoon or pipe buttercream onto the cooled cakes and decorate as desired.

STORE & SHARE *While best eaten on the day they are made, these cakes will keep happily in an airtight container in the fridge for a day or two – just return to room temperature before serving.*

Everything about these sunny little cakes is a joy to me, from the soft orange orb of apricot that sits atop, to the golden saffron-spiked polenta cake below. Serve these on a dainty cake plate with thick (double) cream if you're so inclined, or just eat them greedily, still warm, out of the oven as I invariably seem to do!

Apricot, Polenta & Saffron Tea Cakes

MAKES 12 LITTLE CAKES

Small pinch of saffron threads (approximately ¼ teaspoon, loosely packed)

110 g (3¾ oz) caster (superfine) sugar

1 tablespoon hot water

125 g (4½ oz) unsalted butter, softened, plus extra to grease

1 tablespoon runny honey

1 egg

75 g (2½ oz) self-raising flour

50 g (1¾ oz) fine (instant) polenta

Pinch of fine sea salt

60 ml (2 fl oz) full-cream (whole) milk

6 small ripe apricots, cut in half, pits removed

1 tablespoon Roast Apricot Jam (page 206), or good store-bought apricot jam

Thick (double) cream, to serve (optional)

Preheat the oven to 160°C (325°F) fan-forced and grease a 12-hole muffin/cupcake tin (with 80 ml/2½ fl oz capacity holes) well with butter. Line the bases of the holes with rounds of baking paper, and the sides with strips of baking paper that extend a little above the sides of the tins (fiddly, but necessary, I'm sorry!).

Place the saffron threads and ½ teaspoon of the sugar in a small mortar and pestle and grind until fine. Brush the ground saffron and sugar into a small bowl and pour over the 1 tablespoon of hot water. Cover and set aside to steep while you make the cake batter.

In the bowl of a stand mixer with a paddle attachment, cream the butter, the remaining sugar and the honey until light and fluffy, scraping down the side of the bowl a few times as you go. Add the egg and continue to beat until the mixture is smooth.

Place the self-raising flour, polenta and salt in a separate bowl and use a hand whisk to briefly combine. Add half of the flour mixture to the creamed butter mixture, stirring gently. Combine the steeped saffron mixture with the milk and add half to the batter. Once incorporated, follow with the remaining flour mixture, then the remaining saffron milk, stirring gently until just combined.

Place an apricot half, cut side down, in the base of each hole in the muffin tin. →

Divide the cake batter evenly between the prepared tins, smoothing the tops and tapping the tin gently on the bench a few times to remove any air bubbles.

Bake in the preheated oven for 18–22 minutes or until the cakes are golden brown and cooked through. Allow the cakes to cool in the tin for 5 minutes.

While the cakes are cooling a little, mix the apricot jam with 1 teaspoon of water and heat until bubbling (I do this in a small bowl in the microwave). Remove the strips of baking paper and run a flat-bladed knife around the side of each cake to loosen before carefully inverting them onto a wire rack. Remove the baking paper rounds and brush the tops of the cakes liberally with the hot jam mixture. Allow to cool slightly before serving warm, or at room temperature, with a dollop of cream, if you like.

STORE & SHARE *While best eaten on the day they are made, these little cakes will keep happily in an airtight container in the fridge for a day or two. Warm gently before serving.*

The blackberry brambles by the side of the road are covered in fruit, glimmering in beautiful shades of purple, red and black. I love this time of year, when summer is almost done and autumn starts to furtively show her face around the corner. My cooking turns extra cosy and the thought of a simple bake, to eat straight from the oven with a big pot of tea, is exceptionally appealing. These fruit-studded gems are just the thing; a complete doddle to make and even easier to eat. Do remove the bay leaf from the top of the muffin before you dive in, though – they do rather get stuck in your teeth, and by now they have done their job of perfuming the cake beautifully!

Blackberry, Bay & White Chocolate Muffins

MAKES 12 MUFFINS

200 g (7 oz) wholemeal (whole-wheat) flour

100 g (3½ oz) almond meal

3 teaspoons baking powder

⅛ teaspoon fine sea salt

220 g (7¾ oz) golden (raw) caster (superfine) sugar

180 g (6½ oz) white chocolate, roughly chopped

185 ml (6 fl oz) buttermilk

1½ teaspoons vanilla bean paste

3 eggs

150 g (5½ oz) unsalted butter, melted and cooled

170 g (6 oz) fresh blackberries

12 small fresh bay leaves

Preheat the oven to 170°C (325°F) fan-forced and line two 6-hole large muffin tins (with 180 ml/5¾ fl oz capacity holes) with paper cases.

Place the flour, almond meal, baking powder, salt, sugar and a little more than half the chocolate in a large mixing bowl and use a hand whisk to briefly mix together.

In a separate bowl, combine the buttermilk, vanilla and eggs and whisk well. Make a well in the centre of the dry ingredients and pour in the buttermilk mixture, along with the melted butter. Stir gently with a spoon until just combined (try really hard not to overmix the batter) before dividing evenly between the prepared muffin cases.

Divide the blackberries between the muffins, pressing them gently into the batter, and scatter the remaining white chocolate over the top. Press a bay leaf into the surface of each muffin. Bake in the preheated oven for 20–25 minutes or until the muffins are beautifully golden brown and cooked through. Allow to cool in the tins for 10 minutes before carefully removing from the tin and transferring the muffins to a wire rack to cool further.

STORE & SHARE *These muffins are best served warm or at room temperature on the day they are made, and even better shared outdoors with a flask of something hot! Store any leftovers in an airtight container somewhere cool for a day or two.*

A variation of my mum's beloved sticky date pudding, these little cakes are all warming spice and soft, cooked fruit. With wholemeal flour, sticky prunes and pear, I like to kid myself that these are, in fact, healthy muffins. But then I drown them in ginger caramel and a puddle of cream, and that illusion is shattered! But, can I just say, on a cold evening these really are heavenly. And I wouldn't even blame you if the leftovers masqueraded as breakfast the next day – see above regarding wholemeal flour and fruit. And please, don't be scared off by the prunes, they are lovely in this (I actually prefer them to dates). Just think of them as dried plums if that helps!

Sticky Prune, Pear & Ginger Cakes with Ginger Caramel

MAKES 6 SMALL CAKES

CAKES

100 g (3½ oz) unsalted butter, cubed, plus extra to grease

185 ml (6 fl oz) full-cream (whole) milk

125 g (4½ oz) caster (superfine) sugar

120 g (4¼ oz) pitted prunes, halved

1 teaspoon peeled and finely diced fresh ginger

¼ teaspoon bicarbonate of soda (baking soda)

2 eggs, lightly beaten

1 teaspoon vanilla bean paste

2 small pears, ripe but firm

150 g (5½ oz) wholemeal (whole-wheat) flour, plus extra to dust tins

¾ teaspoon baking powder

¾ teaspoon ground ginger

⅛ teaspoon fine sea salt

Ingredients continued over page

Preheat the oven to 160°C (325°F) fan-forced and grease a 6-hole large muffin tin (with 180 ml/5¾ fl oz capacity holes) well with softened butter. Line the bases of the holes with circles of baking paper, then dust the tins with a little wholemeal flour, tapping out any excess.

Start the cake batter by placing the butter, milk, sugar, prunes and fresh ginger in a medium saucepan. Place over medium heat, stirring occasionally, until the butter has melted and the sugar has dissolved. Remove from the heat, stir in the bicarbonate of soda and allow the mixture to cool to room temperature. When the mixture has cooled, stir in the eggs and vanilla.

While the prune mixture is cooling, peel and quarter the pears, removing the cores. Cut the quarters into 1–2 cm (½–¾ inch) pieces and set aside.

In a large mixing bowl, place the flour, baking powder, ground ginger and fine sea salt, and whisk together. Make a well in the centre and pour in the cooled prune mixture, along with the pear pieces, stirring gently until just combined. Divide the batter evenly between the prepared muffin cups. Bake in the preheated oven for 20–25 minutes or until the cakes are golden brown and risen, and just a few damp crumbs cling to a skewer when tested. Allow the cakes to cool a little in their tins while you make the ginger caramel sauce. →

**STICKY PRUNE, PEAR
& GINGER CAKES WITH
GINGER CARAMEL
CONTINUED**

GINGER CARAMEL SAUCE
100 g (3½ oz) unsalted butter,
   cubed
165 g (5¾ oz) light brown sugar
200 ml (7 fl oz) pure (single)
   cream, plus extra to serve
   (optional)
1 teaspoon peeled and finely
   diced fresh ginger
½ teaspoon flaky sea salt

Place the butter, sugar, cream and ginger in a medium saucepan. Place over medium heat and stir until the butter has melted and the sugar has dissolved. Turn the heat down and let the caramel bubble for 3–5 minutes, stirring occasionally, until slightly thickened, and watching carefully that the caramel doesn't bubble over. Remove from the heat and stir in the flaky sea salt.

Carefully turn the warm cakes out of their tins, running a knife around the edges to loosen if necessary. Serve the cakes warm, topped with warm ginger caramel sauce and a puddle of pure (single) cream, if you like. I like to use a skewer to poke holes in the top of the cakes to allow the caramel sauce to really soak in.

STORE & SHARE *Any left-over cakes and caramel sauce will keep well in an airtight container in the fridge for 2–3 days – just heat gently before serving. I have often gifted a box of these cakes along with an accompanying jar of caramel sauce, with firm instructions to serve warm! It is always well received.*

As demonstrated by the title of my first book, *The Plain Cake Appreciation Society*, my love of plain cakes knows no bounds. And truly, a good pound cake is one of the best plain cakes around. Make them mini, single-serve cakes that one need not share and I think we've really hit the sweet spot!

Below, I've given you a base recipe along with a couple of my favourite seasonal flavour variations – much like one of those choose-your-own-adventure novels. A pot of tea to accompany is, of course, mandatory; but otherwise go forth and bake!

Little Pound Cakes

MAKES 8 SMALL POUND CAKES

200 g (7 oz) unsalted butter, softened, plus extra to grease

200 g (7 oz) caster (superfine) sugar

2 teaspoons vanilla bean paste

3 eggs

200 g (7 oz) plain (all-purpose) flour, plus extra to dust

½ teaspoon baking powder

⅛ teaspoon fine sea salt

80 ml (2½ fl oz) full-cream (whole) milk

Icing (confectioners') sugar, to dust

Preheat the oven to 160°C (325°F) fan-forced. Grease eight 180 ml (5¾ fl oz) capacity mini loaf (bar) tins (or eight large muffin cups, 180 ml/ 5¾ fl oz capacity holes) well with butter and dust with a little flour, tapping out any excess.

In the bowl of a stand mixer with a paddle attachment, cream the butter, caster sugar and vanilla until very light and fluffy. Add the eggs, one at a time, beating well and scraping down the side of the bowl after each addition. Place the flour, baking powder and salt in a separate bowl and use a hand whisk to combine. Add half the dry ingredients to the creamed butter mixture, stirring gently, before adding the milk. Once incorporated, follow with the remaining flour mixture. Scrape down the side of the bowl and stir the batter gently until combined.

Divide the batter evenly between the prepared tins, smoothing the tops and tapping the tins gently on the bench to remove any air bubbles. Bake in the preheated oven for 15–22 minutes or until golden and cooked through. Allow the cakes to cool in their tins for 5 minutes before turning out onto a wire rack to cool further. Serve the cakes a little warm or at room temperature, dusted liberally with icing sugar.

VARIATIONS

RHUBARB & MARMALADE Add 2 tablespoons of fine-cut marmalade to the creamed butter and sugar mixture when making the cake batter, and top each cake with two or three slices of Marmalade Baked Rhubarb (page 213) before baking. →

LEMON & THYME Rub the finely grated zest of 1 lemon and 1 tablespoon of fresh lemon thyme leaves through the caster sugar before creaming it with the butter. Top the cooked cakes with a glaze made by mixing 80 g (2¾ oz) of caster sugar with 1½ tablespoons of lemon juice and some extra lemon thyme leaves. Drizzle over the cakes once you have removed them from their tins, but while they are still warm.

EARL GREY Finely grind 2 teaspoons of Earl Grey tea in a spice grinder or mortar and pestle and add to the creamed butter and sugar mixture along with the finely grated zest of ½ bergamot orange or 1 lemon, when making the cake batter. Top the cooled cakes with a simple icing made by mixing 160 g (5½ oz) pure icing (confectioners') sugar with 1½–2 tablespoons of lemon or bergamot juice.

STORE & SHARE *These little pound cakes make a wonderful gift. I like to box up a selection of flavours and deliver them as a little edible 'hello' or 'happy birthday'! (Include some candles for extra cheer.)*

I love little frangipane tarts with baked quince. Like, a lot. But, sometimes I'm not organised or simply can't be bothered to make a batch of pastry. So why not cut out the middleman, I thought, and just make them sans pastry? One less baking step, and one step closer to my mouth! It was one of my better decisions. And the outcome? Fragrant little (gluten-free) quince-topped cakes. Oh, happy days! Do make the baked quince ahead of time, for a super easy time of it.

Quince & Frangipane Cakes

MAKES 12 LITTLE CAKES * GLUTEN FREE

12 slices of Baked Quince
(page 216)
2 tablespoons flaked almonds
Thick (double) cream, to serve
(optional)

FRANGIPANE
100 g (3½ oz) unsalted butter,
softened, plus extra to grease
110 g (3¾ oz) caster (superfine)
sugar
1 teaspoon vanilla bean paste
Finely grated zest of ½ orange
2 eggs
150 g (5½ oz) almond meal
50 g (1¾ oz) white rice flour,
plus extra to dust
¼ teaspoon baking powder
Pinch of fine sea salt

Preheat the oven to 160°C (325°F) fan-forced and grease a 12-hole muffin/cupcake tin (with 80 ml/2½ fl oz capacity holes), or equivalent, well with softened butter. Dust with a little extra rice flour, tapping out any excess. (Alternatively, line with paper cases.)

To make the frangipane, cream the butter, sugar, vanilla and orange zest in the bowl of a stand mixer with a paddle attachment until light and fluffy. Add the eggs, one at a time, beating well after each addition.

Place the almond meal, rice flour, baking powder and salt in a separate bowl and whisk to combine. Add the dry ingredients to the creamed butter mixture and beat for a minute or so, scraping down the side of the bowl once, until the frangipane is light and fluffy.

Divide the frangipane evenly between the prepared tins and top each cake with a slice of baked quince, curling the slices into a smile to fit inside the tins. Sprinkle with the flaked almonds and bake in the preheated oven for 18–22 minutes or until the frangipane is golden and cooked through. Allow the cakes to cool in the tins for 10 minutes before carefully turning them out and serving warm or at room temperature. A dollop of thick cream wouldn't go astray here.

STORE & SHARE *Store any left-over cakes in an airtight container in the fridge for 2–3 days. Return to room temperature or warm slightly before serving.*

Madeleines; a perennial favourite in our house. The flavour may change according to the season or our particular whim, but they are firmly cemented as a winner around here. This combination of flavours – cardamom, bay and orange – feels particularly right in the depths of winter, when I want a little spice and a small, sweet treat with my morning cup. Owing to their simple melt-and-mix batter, they are no great hardship to make – and when they emerge from their tins, delicately scalloped and impossibly cute, I'm won over every time!

Cardamom, Bay & Orange Madeleines

MAKES ABOUT 24 MADELEINES

125 g (4½ oz) unsalted butter, plus extra to grease

2 tablespoons (40 ml/1¼ fl oz) full-cream (whole) milk

2 fresh bay leaves

1 tablespoon runny honey

110 g (3¾ oz) caster (superfine) sugar

2 eggs

125 g (4½ oz) plain (all-purpose) flour, plus extra to dust

1 teaspoon baking powder

½ teaspoon ground cardamom

Pinch of fine sea salt

ORANGE GLAZE

240 g (8¾ oz) pure icing (confectioners') sugar, sifted

Finely grated zest of ½ orange

3 tablespoons (60 ml/2 fl oz) fresh orange juice

Place the butter, milk, bay leaves and honey in a small saucepan and place over low heat. Stir gently until the butter has melted and the honey has dissolved. Remove from the heat and set aside to cool.

When the butter mixture is cool, place the caster sugar in a medium mixing bowl along with the eggs and use a hand whisk to mix until well combined. Place the flour, baking powder, ground cardamom and salt in a separate bowl and mix briefly to combine. Add the dry ingredients to the egg and sugar mixture and whisk until smooth. Finally, remove the bay leaves from the cooled butter mixture and whisk this into the batter too, taking care not to overmix. Cover the bowl and place the batter in the fridge to chill for at least 2 hours (or up to 2 days).

When the batter has chilled, preheat the oven to 170°C (325°F) fan-forced and brush two 12-hole madeleine tins well with softened butter. Dust the tins with a little plain flour, tapping out any excess. Spoon a scant tablespoon of batter into each madeleine hole, filling them about two-thirds full. Bake in the preheated oven for 8–10 minutes or until the madeleines have risen and are deep golden around the edges.

While the cakes are cooking, make the orange glaze by combining the icing sugar, orange zest and 2 tablespoons of the orange juice in a mixing bowl. Stir until smooth, adding enough of the remaining orange juice to form a nice drippy glaze. It needs to be quite loose, so it delicately coats the madeleines, without overwhelming the flavour of the cake. →

When the cakes are cooked, allow them to cool for a minute or two in the tins, then remove the madeleines, one by one, and spoon a little glaze over each. Place on a wire rack set over a baking tray to catch any drips. Allow the glaze to set before serving with a big pot of tea.

STORE & SHARE *The madeleines are best eaten on the day they are made. However, the uncooked batter will keep happily in the fridge for a day or two, so you can bake them in batches as the need arises – a delightful thing to be able to do when friends drop by for tea!*

For me, a small cake is a pleasure far greater than its size would suggest. And this simple, sunny combination of passionfruit and coconut is one of my favourites. It feels particularly Australian – and speaks to sunshiny days spent outdoors. Sometimes I make a batch of these in the depths of winter, when it's cold and dark outside – and the making and eating never fails to bring a little handful of sunshine!

Coconut & Passionfruit Loaves

MAKES 8 LITTLE LOAVES

LOAVES

A little plain (all-purpose) flour, to dust

150 g (5½ oz) unsalted butter, softened, plus extra to grease

200 g (7 oz) golden (raw) caster (superfine) sugar

1½ teaspoons vanilla bean paste

3 eggs

150 g (5½ oz) self-raising flour, plus extra to dust

80 g (2¾ oz) fine desiccated coconut

⅛ teaspoon fine sea salt

125 ml (4 fl oz) buttermilk

PASSIONFRUIT ICING (FROSTING)

160 g (5½ oz) pure icing (confectioners') sugar, sifted

2 tablespoons fresh passionfruit pulp (1–2 passionfruit)

Preheat the oven to 160°C (325°F) fan-forced, and grease eight 180 ml (5¾ fl oz) capacity mini loaf (bar) tins (or eight large muffin cups, 180 ml/ 5¾ fl oz capacity holes) well with butter and dust with a little flour, tapping out any excess.

In the bowl of a stand mixer with a paddle attachment, cream the butter, caster sugar and vanilla until very light and fluffy. Add the eggs, one at a time, beating well after each addition. Continue to beat, scraping down the side of the bowl once or twice, until all the egg is incorporated and the mixture is creamy.

Place the self-raising flour, coconut and salt in a separate bowl and use a hand whisk to briefly combine. Add half to the creamed butter mixture, stirring gently, before adding half the buttermilk. Once incorporated, follow with the remaining flour mixture, then the remaining buttermilk, stirring gently until combined.

Divide the batter between the prepared tins, smoothing the tops and tapping the tins gently on the bench a few times to remove any air bubbles. Bake in the preheated oven for 15–20 minutes or until the cakes are golden, risen and cooked through. Allow the cakes to cool in the tin for 10 minutes before carefully turning them out onto a wire rack to cool completely. →

**COCONUT &
PASSIONFRUIT
LOAVES CONTINUED**

When the cakes are cool, make the passionfruit icing by combining the icing sugar and 1½ tablespoons of the passionfruit pulp in a mixing bowl. Stir until the mixture is smooth, then add enough of the remaining passionfruit pulp so that you have a nice drippy consistency.

Spoon the icing over the cooled cakes, allowing it to drip down the sides. Set the cakes aside for the icing to set before serving – or don't! Just eat them straight away with a big pot of strong black tea. Heaven.

STORE & SHARE *These little cakes are, of course, best eaten on the day they are made, but they will keep happily in an airtight container in a cool place for 2–3 days.*

I like to think of these sunny little cakes as the summer version of a Victoria sponge – all tropical fruit and fluffy, sweet cream. These make the perfect small summertime dessert, eaten outside when the weather is soft and balmy, and mangoes are sweet and plentiful. Clouds of passionfruit-spiked whipped cream hold the whole delightful show together.

Mango & Passionfruit Cream Cakes

MAKES 12 SMALL CAKES

CAKES

A little plain (all-purpose) flour, to dust

250 g (9 oz) unsalted butter, softened, plus extra to grease

300 g (10½ oz) caster (superfine) sugar

Finely grated zest of 1 lime

1 teaspoon vanilla bean paste

4 eggs

200 g (7 oz) self-raising flour

50 g (1¾ oz) custard powder

⅛ teaspoon fine sea salt

125 ml (4 fl oz) full-cream (whole) milk

FILLING

300 ml (10½ fl oz) thickened (whipping) cream

1 teaspoon vanilla bean paste

1 tablespoon icing (confectioners') sugar mixture, plus extra to dust

Ingredients continued over page

Preheat the oven to 160°C (325°F) fan-forced and grease two 6-hole large muffin tins (with 180 ml/5¾ fl oz capacity holes) well with softened butter. I have a tin with straight-sided cups, which looks lovely, but these taste just as good baked in regular large muffin tins. Dust the tins with a little plain flour, tapping out any excess.

In the bowl of a stand mixer with a paddle attachment, cream the butter, caster sugar, lime zest and vanilla until very light and fluffy. Add the eggs, one at a time, beating well and scraping down the side of the bowl after each addition.

Place the flour, custard powder and salt in a separate bowl and use a hand whisk to combine. Add half to the creamed butter mixture, stirring gently, before adding half the milk. Scrape down the side of the bowl, then follow with the remaining flour mixture and the remaining milk, stirring gently until just combined.

Divide the batter between the prepared tins, smoothing the tops and tapping the tins gently on the bench a few times to remove any air bubbles. Bake in the preheated oven for 15–20 minutes or until the cakes are risen and cooked through. Allow the cakes to cool in the tins for 10 minutes before carefully turning out onto a wire rack to cool completely.

When the cakes are cool, whip the thickened cream, vanilla and icing sugar together to firm peaks. Add the passionfruit curd and half the passionfruit pulp and fold them through, then set aside. →

2 tablespoons Passionfruit Curd
   (page 210), or good store-
   bought passionfruit curd
80 ml (2½ fl oz) fresh passionfruit
   pulp (from 4–5 passionfruit)
1 large ripe mango, peeled and
   diced
Finely grated zest and juice of
   ½ lime

In a bowl, stir the remaining passionfruit pulp through the diced mango, along with the lime zest and a generous squeeze of lime juice.

Place the cakes on a serving plate. Split in half, and top the bottom halves with a generous scoop of the passionfruit cream. Use the back of a spoon to create a little nest in the cream, then place a spoonful of the mango and passionfruit mixture into each nest. Gently sandwich the tops of the cakes on and dust liberally with icing sugar. (Alternatively, you can leave the cakes unsplit and simply pile the cream and fruit on top.)

STORE & SHARE *These little cakes are best shared outdoors with friends, soon after assembling. Store any leftovers in an airtight container in the fridge for a day or so, returning to room temperature before eating.*

I am a total sucker for just about any version of a Victoria sponge. Plain cake, jam and cream – what more could you want? But make them little, individual Victorias and you really have my attention. The beauty of this recipe lies in its simplicity. These little cakes are made with cream, not butter, in the batter, meaning that you can mix them all in one bowl, by hand. And anything that gets me closer to a cake with less effort is a win in my book! Filling them with whipped yoghurt-cream and homemade jam really does make them sing, but any good jam you are in possession of will do the trick!

Strawberry & Rhubarb Jam Victoria Sponges

MAKES 6 LITTLE CAKES

CAKES

Unsalted butter, to grease

A little plain (all-purpose) flour, to dust

200 ml (7 fl oz) thick (double) cream

165 g (5¾ oz) caster (superfine) sugar

1 teaspoon vanilla bean paste

2 eggs

150 g (5½ oz) self-raising flour

⅛ teaspoon fine sea salt

TO FILL

200 ml (7 fl oz) thickened (whipping) cream

100 g (3½ oz) Greek-style yoghurt

1 tablespoon icing (confectioners') sugar mixture, plus extra to dust

1 teaspoon rosewater

160 g (5½ oz) Strawberry & Rhubarb Jam (page 211)

Preheat the oven to 160°C (325°F) fan-forced and grease a 6-hole large muffin tin (with 180 ml/5¾ fl oz capacity holes) well with softened butter. I have a tin with straight-sided cups, which looks lovely, but a regular large muffin tin works just as well. Dust the tin with a little plain flour, tapping out any excess.

Make the cake batter by placing the cream, sugar and vanilla in a large mixing bowl and using a hand whisk to combine. Do not overmix or the cream will become too stiff. Add the eggs, one at a time, whisking after each addition. Add the self-raising flour and salt to the bowl, and whisk briefly to form a smooth batter.

Divide the batter evenly between the prepared tins, smoothing the tops with a spatula and tapping the tins gently on the bench to remove any air bubbles. Bake in the preheated oven for 15–20 minutes or until the cakes have risen and are cooked through. Allow the cakes to cool in their tins for 10 minutes before carefully turning them out onto a wire rack to cool completely.

When ready to assemble the cakes, make the filling by whipping the cream, yoghurt, sugar and rosewater to soft peaks. Split the cakes in half, and top the bottom halves with a generous scoop of the cream mixture. Use the back of a spoon to create a little nest in the cream, then place a spoonful of jam on top. Gently sandwich the tops of the cakes on and dust liberally with icing sugar.

STORE & SHARE *These cakes are best served soon after assembling.*

Essentially a friand, these little gluten-free, blueberry-studded cakes are a real pleasure. Especially eaten just warm from the oven, when the blueberries burst juicily on your tongue and the flaked coconut is crisp and toasty. When I was a waitress at a local cafe as a teenager, a latte in a tall glass and a friand were the height of sophistication – I'm no longer sure that's true of the latte, but I think it is high time we brought back the friand!

Blueberry, Coconut & Lemon Bars

MAKES 12 LITTLE CAKES * GLUTEN FREE

80 g (2¾ oz) almond meal

80 g (2¾ oz) desiccated coconut

50 g (1¾ oz) white rice flour, plus extra to dust

½ teaspoon baking powder

Pinch of fine sea salt

120 g (4¼ oz) pure icing (confectioners') sugar, sifted

4 egg whites (140 g/5 oz)

1 teaspoon vanilla bean paste

Finely grated zest of 1 lemon

100 g (3½ oz) unsalted butter, melted and cooled, plus extra to grease

125 g (4½ oz) fresh blueberries

4 tablespoons (30 g/1 oz) flaked coconut

Preheat the oven to 160°C (325°F) fan-forced and grease a 12-hole tiny loaf (bar) or muffin/cupcake tin (with 80 ml/2½ fl oz capacity holes) well with softened butter. Dust with a little extra rice flour, tapping out any excess.

Place the almond meal, desiccated coconut, white rice flour, baking powder, salt and sugar in a mixing bowl and use a hand whisk to combine.

In a separate bowl, use a hand whisk to whisk the egg whites until frothy. Add the whisked egg whites to the dry ingredients along with the vanilla, lemon zest and melted butter. Stir until smooth.

Divide the batter evenly between the prepared tins. Next, divide the blueberries between the cakes, gently pressing them into the batter, then top with the flaked coconut. Bake in the preheated oven for 20–25 minutes or until the cakes are cooked through and the coconut flakes are golden. Allow the cakes to cool in the tins for 10 minutes before carefully turning them out onto a wire rack to cool completely.

STORE & SHARE *These little cakes will keep well in an airtight container in the fridge for a day or two – just return them to room temperature before serving.*

Don't let their somewhat underwhelming appearance fool you – these rich, intensely chocolatey, little cheesecakes really are heavenly! Serve them at room temperature, when they are beautifully soft, with a spoonful of cream in their sunken little tops, or a smattering of sharp, fresh raspberries (or both!), and thank me later. Creamy and decadent, they are just as a cheesecake ought to be.

Sunken Chocolate Cheesecakes

MAKES 12 LITTLE CAKES * GLUTEN FREE

500 g (1 lb 2 oz) cream cheese, at room temperature

250 g (9 oz) dark chocolate (45–55% cocoa solids), melted

165 g (5¾ oz) caster (superfine) sugar

⅛ teaspoon fine sea salt

3 teaspoons vanilla bean paste

4 eggs

200 g (7 oz) sour cream

2 tablespoons (20 g/¾ oz) Dutch-process (unsweetened) cocoa powder, plus extra to dust (optional)

1 tablespoon gluten-free cornflour (cornstarch)

Preheat the oven to 210°C (400°F) fan-forced and line two 6-hole large muffin tins (with 180 ml/5¾ fl oz capacity holes) with paper muffin wrappers. You need the tulip-shaped wrappers that extend up above the top of the tins (or make your own using squares of baking paper), as the cheesecakes will rise quite a bit while cooking.

Place the cream cheese in the bowl of a stand mixer with a paddle attachment and mix until smooth. Add the warm melted chocolate and mix on low speed until combined. Scrape down the side of the bowl and add the sugar, salt and vanilla, mixing again until smooth. Add the eggs, one at a time, mixing well and scraping down the side of the bowl after each addition.

In a separate bowl, mix the sour cream until smooth. Sift in the cocoa and cornflour and mix again until smooth. Add this to the cream cheese and chocolate mixture and mix on low speed, scraping down the side of the bowl once or twice, until smooth.

Strain the batter through a sieve into a large jug, discarding any lumps, then divide evenly among the prepared muffin cups. Tap the tins gently on the bench a few times to remove any large air bubbles. Bake in the preheated oven for 10–14 minutes or until the surfaces of the cakes are set and starting to crack, but they are still wobbly in the middle. They cook further as they cool, and it's better to err on the side of undercooked rather than overcooked with such small cakes. →

Allow the cakes to cool to room temperature in the tins before serving, or place in the fridge for a couple of hours or overnight to chill. Dust with extra cocoa just before serving, if you like.

Return to room temperature before serving if you like a creamy, soft cheesecake, or serve cold, straight from the fridge, if you prefer something a little more dense.

STORE & SHARE *These rich little cakes can be prepared the day before you want to serve them as they keep very happily in the fridge for a day or two.*

I've learnt, through much trial and error, that there really is no quick or clean way of coating lamingtons. You just have to accept that melted chocolate and coconut (and in this case hazelnuts) will end up all over the place – if you are really lucky, some of it may even end up on your cakes! But mess aside, homemade lamingtons would have to be one of the most joyful bakes around. My children really love them – and at the end of a long day, or a particularly trying week, a plate of these eaten on the verandah, watching the kids lark around, chocolate liberally smeared on their faces, really does make it all seem worthwhile.

Hazelnut Lamington Fingers

MAKES ONE 20 CM (8 INCH) SQUARE CAKE (18 LAMINGTONS)

CAKE

185 g (6½ oz) unsalted butter, softened

200 g (7 oz) caster (superfine) sugar

1 teaspoon vanilla bean paste

3 eggs

175 g (6 oz) self-raising flour

75 g (2½ oz) ground hazelnuts

½ teaspoon baking powder

⅛ teaspoon fine sea salt

150 ml (5 fl oz) buttermilk

200 g (7 oz) store-bought chocolate hazelnut spread

CHOCOLATE GLAZE

225 g (8 oz) dark chocolate (45–55% cocoa solids), chopped

20 g (¾ oz) unsalted butter

185 ml (6 fl oz) full-cream (whole) milk

Ingredients continued over page

Preheat the oven to 160°C (325°F) fan-forced. Line the base and sides of a 20 cm (8 inch) square cake tin with baking paper.

In the bowl of a stand mixer with a paddle attachment, cream the butter, sugar and vanilla until very light and fluffy. Add the eggs, one at a time, scraping down the side of the bowl and beating well after each addition.

Place the flour, ground hazelnuts, baking powder and salt in a separate bowl and use a hand whisk to combine. Add half the dry ingredients to the creamed butter mixture, stirring gently, before adding half the buttermilk. Once incorporated, follow with the remaining dry ingredients, then the remaining buttermilk, stirring gently until combined.

Spoon the batter into the prepared tin, smoothing the top with a spatula and tapping the tin gently on the bench a few times to remove any air bubbles. Bake in the preheated oven for 30–35 minutes or until the cake is golden and cooked through. Allow the cake to cool in the tin for 10 minutes or so before turning out onto a wire rack to cool completely.

When the cake is cool, make the chocolate glaze by combining the chocolate, butter and milk in a small saucepan over very low heat. Cook, stirring often, with a hand whisk, until the chocolate and butter have melted and the glaze is smooth. Set aside to cool slightly while you slice and fill the cake. →

100 g (3½ oz) roasted hazelnuts
(see page 9), chopped
120 g (4¼ oz) shredded coconut
100 g (3½ oz) flaked coconut

Use a large, serrated knife to slice the cooled cake in half, horizontally, so you have two thinner layers. Top the bottom layer with the chocolate hazelnut spread, smoothing it out into an even layer. Sandwich the top layer on and press it gently down into place. Cut the cake into 18 small bars. Pour the chopped roasted hazelnuts and the shredded and flaked coconut into a large shallow bowl and mix well. Carefully coat the cakes in the warm chocolate glaze, then toss them gently in the hazelnut and coconut mixture. Place the cakes on a baking tray scattered with a little extra coconut and allow the glaze to firm a little before serving.

STORE & SHARE *While best eaten the day they are made, these little cakes will keep happily in an airtight container in a cool place for 2–3 days.*

This is where I come for comfort. Pillowy, buttery solace. This is my childhood in edible form. Soothing spiced bread, frying butter and dollops of jam and cream. Fresh, warm scones and carbohydrate-induced succour. Bottomless pots of tea. Sticky fingers and soft, sweet buns to share.

When the weather sets in or my head is a little foggy, there is something particular I crave – yeasted dough. I want to meditatively mix and knead and watch patiently as the silky dough rises. I want to shape it, adding layers of sugar, spice and butter, and fold it into buns. Because a light, fluffy, sugary bun is the ultimate in restorative baking. Love in bread form.

Sugared Scones, Pikelets & Sticky Buns

As the saying goes, these pikelets (or drop scones) are not 'rocket science' – instead, they are quick, easy and deeply comforting. A family staple, both of my childhood and now that of my children, pikelets are on high rotation at our house. In fact, I'm not sure any of us would have survived the baby-haze-days after Kip was born without the sustenance and activity of making these. Indeed, they are still our go-to breakfast or afternoon tea when things feel a little too much. They're a complete doddle to prepare and I find the smell of frying butter infinitely soothing. Serve warm with butter and jam (or cream if you like, my kids like!). Equally popular with small and big people alike.

Buttermilk Pikelets

MAKES ABOUT 24 PIKELETS

2 eggs

300 ml (10½ fl oz) buttermilk

200 g (7 oz) self-raising flour

Unsalted or salted butter, to fry
   and serve

Good jam, to serve

Whipped or thick (double) cream,
   to serve (optional)

Place the eggs and buttermilk in a medium mixing bowl and use a hand whisk to combine. Sift in the flour and whisk again until smooth. Set aside.

Place a large non-stick frying pan over medium heat. Add about 2 teaspoons of butter and heat until bubbling, swirling it around to coat the base of the pan. Drop tablespoonfuls of batter into the pan, leaving plenty of room between the pikelets so you can easily turn them over.

Cook for 2 minutes or so, or until bubbles start to appear on the surface of the pikelets. Use a non-stick spatula or egg slice to turn the pikelets over, cooking for a further minute until both sides are golden brown around the edges. Remove the pikelets from the pan and serve straight away, or keep them warm while you continue to cook the rest of the pikelets, in batches. Add more butter to fry in as necessary, until all the batter has been used. Keep an eye on the heat and turn it down to low if the pikelets are browning too quickly.

Serve the pikelets warm from the pan with butter and jam, or jam and cream, if you like – and revel in the nostalgia of childhood!

STORE & SHARE *These pikelets make a great addition to a picnic tea. We often take a batch (wrapped in foil to keep warm) along with a jar of jam and one of cream, to the park or a friend's house to eat in the sunshine. Most cheering! Store any leftovers in the fridge for a day or two, but really, there probably won't be any!*

There is something extremely soothing about these coconut buns. They are overt in neither flavour nor appearance, but rather beguiling in their simplicity – their appealingly soft, white and beige colour palette singing comfort in the extreme. Eaten warm from the oven, with a cup of scalding hot tea, I can think of little better. They are lightly sweet and fragrant with coconut, in both the dough and frangipane-like filling. Only one rule here: they must be eaten warm!

Coconut Buns

MAKES 6 BUNS

BUNS

250 g (9 oz) bread flour, plus extra to dust

55 g (2 oz) caster (superfine) sugar

7 g (¼ oz) instant dried yeast

1 teaspoon vanilla bean paste

125 ml (4 fl oz) milk, just warm

½ teaspoon fine sea salt

1 egg, lightly beaten, for the dough, plus 1 egg, well beaten, for glaze

60 g (2¼ oz) unsalted butter, softened

60 g (2¼ oz) desiccated coconut

Pearl sugar, to decorate (optional)

Ingredients continued over page

First, start making the bun dough by placing 50 g (1¾ oz) of the flour, 2 teaspoons of the caster sugar and the yeast in a medium mixing bowl. In a small jug, mix the vanilla into the just warm milk and add 60 ml (2 fl oz) of this to the flour, sugar and yeast mixture. Stir to a smooth paste, cover and set aside for 45–60 minutes somewhere warm, until the mixture is bubbly and light. What we're doing here is a type of pre-ferment, which improves the flavour and texture of the cooked dough, making it softer and lighter. It also makes the dough less sticky and easier to work with when shaping. You can skip this step if you are short on time, but I think it's worth doing if you can.

When the pre-ferment is ready, place the remaining 200 g (7 oz) of flour, the remaining caster sugar and the salt in the bowl of a stand mixer with a dough hook. Add the remaining milk and vanilla mixture, along with the pre-ferment and the lightly beaten egg. Mix on low speed until combined, then increase the speed to medium and continue to mix for 8–10 minutes, until the dough is elastic and starting to pull away from the side of the bowl.

Add the softened butter, 1 tablespoon at a time, mixing until all the butter is incorporated. Once the butter is incorporated, add the desiccated coconut and continue to mix on medium speed for 6–8 minutes more, scraping down the side of the bowl once or twice, or until the dough is shiny and has pulled away from the side of the bowl. This is a soft dough, so it may not ball cleanly; rather you are looking for it to be stretchy and elastic and to no longer stick to your fingers when pinched. →

COCONUT BUNS
CONTINUED

COCONUT FRANGIPANE
FILLING

60 g (2¼ oz) unsalted butter,
  very soft
55 g (2 oz) caster (superfine)
  sugar
½ teaspoon vanilla bean paste
1 egg, lightly beaten
2 tablespoons plain (all-purpose)
  flour
80 g (2¾ oz) desiccated coconut
Pinch of fine sea salt

Use buttered hands to transfer the dough to a well-buttered bowl, cover with plastic wrap and place somewhere warm to prove until light and almost doubled in size, 1–2 hours (or you can slow-prove the dough in the fridge overnight if you want to bake the buns the next morning).

While the dough is proving, make the frangipane filling by combining the softened butter, sugar and vanilla in a mixing bowl. Beat with a wooden spoon until light and creamy. Add the egg, flour, desiccated coconut and the salt, and mix again until smooth. Cover and set aside.

When the dough has risen, line a 6-hole large muffin tin (with 180 ml/5¾ fl oz capacity holes) with paper cases.

Gently press the air out of the dough and place it on a clean work surface, lightly dusted with flour. Using a rolling pin or your hands, press or roll the dough out to a 30 cm (12 inch) square. Spread the surface evenly with coconut frangipane filling. Starting at the side closest to you, roll the dough away from you into a log, making sure the seam finishes underneath. Use a sharp knife to cut it into six equal pieces. Place one slice, spiral facing up, in each muffin case. Set aside, covered lightly with plastic wrap, to prove again somewhere warm for 30–60 minutes until the buns are light and risen.

While the buns are proving, preheat the oven to 170°C (325°F) fan-forced.

When risen, brush the buns with the extra beaten egg and sprinkle with pearl sugar (if using), before placing in the preheated oven to bake for 15–20 minutes or until golden, springy and cooked through.

STORE & SHARE *These buns are at their best eaten warm from the oven on the day they are baked. Store any leftovers in an airtight container for a day or two, but be sure to reheat them gently before serving.*

Fresh, warm scones are one of those rare foods that have the power to restore your faith in humanity just a little, I think. Eaten with a wedge of melting butter and good company, they really do take the edge off a bad day.

When I worked in a tea shop, most mornings on my way into work I used to pick up a date scone from the bakery next door. Starting the day, scone in hand as I brewed the teas, was really one of my favourite things. These scones, with a healthy dose of soft, sweet dates and a warming hum courtesy of fresh ginger, really are very excellent with a pot of tea. Eat them warm, with lots of butter.

Date & Ginger Scones

MAKES 8 SCONES

150 g (5½ oz) wholemeal (whole-wheat) flour, plus extra to dust
75 g (2½ oz) self-raising flour
1½ teaspoons baking powder
50 g (1¾ oz) unsalted butter, cold, cubed
¼ teaspoon fine sea salt
2 teaspoons caster (superfine) sugar
80 g (2¾ oz) pitted dates, roughly chopped
1 teaspoon peeled and finely diced fresh ginger
160 ml (5¼ fl oz) buttermilk, plus extra to glaze
1 egg, lightly beaten
1 tablespoon raw (demerara) sugar, to sprinkle
Salted butter, to serve

Preheat the oven to 190°C (375°F) fan-forced and line a baking tray with baking paper.

Place the wholemeal flour, self-raising flour and baking powder in a large mixing bowl, and mix briefly. Scatter in the cold cubed butter and mix again to coat all the pieces in flour. Then, using your fingertips, rub the butter into the flour until the mixture resembles coarse breadcrumbs.

Add the salt, caster sugar, chopped dates and diced ginger and stir them through. Make a well in the centre of the dry ingredients and pour in the buttermilk and egg. Use a butter knife to gently mix the wet ingredients into the dry ingredients. When the dough starts to come together into a shaggy mass, use your hands to knead the dough briefly in the bowl until it comes together in a ball. It will be quite soft and sticky.

Tip the dough out on a well-floured surface. Dust the top of the dough with flour too, then gently fold and knead the dough a couple of times before shaping it into a fat round (about 2.5 cm/1 inch thick) with your hands. Use a floured 6 cm (2½ inch) round scone cutter to cut out as many scones as you can, making sure not to twist the cutter as you cut the scones. Gather up the offcuts and pat out again, cutting out remaining scones. →

Place the scones close together on the prepared tray. Brush the tops with a little extra buttermilk and sprinkle liberally with raw sugar. Bake in the preheated oven for 15–18 minutes or until the tops are deep golden, and the scones are cooked through. Allow the scones to cool for 10 minutes before serving them warm, split with lots of cold butter.

STORE & SHARE *If you're not serving the scones straight away, wrap the hot scones in a clean tea towel (dish towel) to keep them warm until ready to serve. Wrapped like this they also make a most excellent portable morning or afternoon tea – just be sure to remember the butter! Store any leftovers in an airtight container at room temperature to eat the next day, but please do reheat them before serving.*

As mentioned in my Date & Ginger Scones recipe (page 158), I find a good scone rather life-affirming – and I must say, I do love these lemon ones. They are fluffy and light courtesy of the buttermilk, with a lovely soft citrus flavour. If you have some Roast Apricot Jam (page 206) or Passionfruit Curd (page 210), you are in for a real treat; but if not, they are also very good with any fine jam you have on hand.

I have to admit too, I have a particularly soft spot for scones. In the first few months after my son was born, at every opportunity we'd bundle him up and trundle off to the nearest establishment in the mountains serving Devonshire tea. Olive, Slav and I would sit hoovering scones and tea in the sunshine while Kip snoozed in his capsule. The scones weren't always the best, but the memories are.

Sugared Buttermilk & Lemon Scones

MAKES 8 SCONES

1½ tablespoons (30 g/1 oz) caster (superfine) sugar, plus extra to top

Finely grated zest of 1 lemon

250 g (9 oz) self-raising flour, plus extra to dust

60 g (2¼ oz) unsalted butter, cold, cubed

¼ teaspoon fine sea salt

1 egg, separated

150 ml (5 fl oz) buttermilk

Thick (double) cream, to serve

Roast Apricot Jam (page 206) or Passionfruit Curd (page 210), to serve, or other good jam

Preheat the oven to 190°C (375°F) fan-forced and line a baking tray with baking paper.

First, place the sugar and lemon zest in a small bowl and use your fingertips to rub the zest through the sugar until fragrant. Set aside.

Place the flour in a large mixing bowl, and scatter in the cold cubed butter. Mix briefly, to coat all the pieces in flour then, using your fingertips, rub the butter into the flour until the mixture resembles coarse breadcrumbs.

Add the salt and the sugar and lemon mixture to the bowl with the flour and butter and stir them through. Mix the egg yolk into the buttermilk, then make a well in the centre of the dry ingredients and pour in the buttermilk mixture. Use a butter knife to gently mix the wet ingredients into the dry. When the dough starts to come together into a shaggy mass, use your hands to knead the dough briefly in the bowl until it comes together. Add a tiny bit of extra buttermilk here if necessary.

Tip the dough out on a lightly floured surface, then gently fold the dough a couple of times before shaping it into a rectangle about 2 cm (¾ inch) in thickness. Use a floured 5 cm (2 inch) round cutter to cut out as many scones as you can, making sure not to twist the cutter as you cut the scones. Gather up the offcuts and pat out again, cutting out the remaining scones. →

Place the scones close together in a round on the prepared tray. Whisk the reserved egg white with a fork until frothy, before brushing it over the tops of the scones. Sprinkle generously with the extra sugar and bake in the preheated oven for 12–15 minutes or until the tops are deep golden, and the scones are cooked through. Allow the scones to cool for 10 minutes before serving them warm, split with lots of cream and jam or curd.

If not serving the scones straight away, wrap the hot scones in a clean tea towel (dish towel) to keep them warm until ready to serve.

STORE & SHARE *The scones are best eaten warm on the day they are made. Store any leftovers in an airtight container at room temperature for a day or two, but please do reheat them before serving!*

I'm not sure when cardamom buns snuck into our family's Christmas traditions, but I am so glad they did. For some time now, they have played an integral role in our festive morning activities – bridging the hungry gap between being woken at an ungodly hour by small folk, and proper Christmas breakfast (naturally eaten at lunchtime). We eat these, bleary-eyed, hot tea in hand, while the kids tear paper from presents and up-end Christmas stockings. This little pocket of time is perhaps my favourite.

Don't relegate these solely to the 'festive bake' category; they really are good any time of year. My daughter likes hers filled with chocolate hazelnut spread rather than spiced filling which, I have to say, I'm partial too also – this feels particularly right at Easter. To make a chocolate version, simply replace the spiced filling with 300 g (10½ oz) chocolate hazelnut spread.

Cardamom Tea Buns

MAKES 12 BUNS

BUNS

250 ml (9 fl oz) full-cream (whole) milk

1 teaspoon ground cardamom

1 teaspoon vanilla bean paste

2 teaspoons English Breakfast tea leaves (or similar)

500 g (1 lb 2 oz) bread flour, plus extra to dust

80 g (2¾ oz) caster (superfine) sugar

10 g (¼ oz) instant dried yeast

½ teaspoon fine sea salt

2 eggs, lightly beaten

125 g (4½ oz) unsalted butter, softened

Ingredients continued over page

To make the buns, first place the milk, cardamom and vanilla in a small saucepan. Place over low heat and bring to just below a simmer. Remove from the heat and set aside to cool until just warm. While the milk is cooling, place the tea leaves in a small spice grinder or mortar and pestle and grind until fine. Set aside.

When the milk is just warm, start the dough by placing 100 g (3½ oz) of the flour, 1 tablespoon of the sugar and the yeast in a medium mixing bowl. Add 125 ml (4 fl oz) of the warm milk mixture to the bowl and stir to a smooth paste. Cover and set aside for 45–60 minutes somewhere warm, until the mixture is bubbly and light. What we're doing here is a type of pre-ferment, which improves the flavour and texture of the cooked dough, making it softer and lighter. It also makes the dough less sticky and easier to work with when shaping. You can skip this step if you are short on time, but I think it's worth doing if you can.

When the pre-ferment is ready, place the remaining 400 g (14 oz) of flour, the remaining sugar, the salt and ground tea in the bowl of a stand mixer with a dough hook. Add the remaining milk mixture, as well as the pre-ferment and eggs, and mix on low speed until combined. Increase the speed to medium and continue to mix for 8–10 minutes until the dough is elastic and pulling away from the side of the bowl. Add the softened butter, 1 tablespoon at a time, and knead again until all the butter is incorporated. →

CARDAMOM TEA BUNS
CONTINUED

SPICED BUTTER FILLING

125 g (4½ oz) unsalted butter,
   very soft

55 g (2 oz) light brown sugar

55 g (2 oz) caster (superfine)
   sugar

2 teaspoons ground cinnamon

½ teaspoon ground cardamom

1 teaspoon vanilla bean paste

Pinch of fine sea salt

60 g (2¼ oz) almond meal

SUGAR GLAZE

55 g (2 oz) caster (superfine)
   sugar

1 teaspoon English Breakfast tea
   leaves

60 ml (2 fl oz) boiling water

Continue to knead for 6–8 minutes more or until the dough is shiny and smooth and has pulled away from the side of the bowl. This is a pretty wet dough so don't expect it to ball cleanly; rather you are looking for it to be stretchy and elastic, and to no longer stick to your fingers when pinched. Use buttered hands to transfer the dough to a well-buttered bowl and cover with plastic wrap. Place somewhere warm and allow to prove until doubled in size, 1–2 hours (or you can slow-prove the dough in the fridge overnight if you want to bake the buns the next morning).

While the dough is proving, make the spiced butter filling by combining all the ingredients in a mixing bowl. Use a wooden spoon to mix well until smooth and light. Set aside.

When the dough has risen, line two 6-hole large muffin tins (with 180 ml/5¾ fl oz capacity holes) with paper cases. Gently press the air out of the dough and place it on a clean work surface, lightly dusted with flour. Using a rolling pin, or your hands, press or roll the dough out to a rectangle roughly 60 x 30 cm (24 x 12 inches). Spread evenly with the spiced butter filling (or 300 g/10½ oz chocolate hazelnut spread). Starting with the long side closest to you, roll the dough away from you into a log, making sure the seam finishes underneath. Use a sharp knife to cut it into 12 equal pieces. Place one slice, spiral facing up, in each muffin case. Set aside, covered lightly with plastic wrap, to prove again somewhere warm for 30–60 minutes until the buns are light and risen.

While the buns are proving, preheat the oven to 180°C (350°F) fan-forced. When the buns have risen, bake in the preheated oven for 15–20 minutes or until golden brown and cooked through.

While the buns are cooking, make the sugar glaze by combining the sugar and tea leaves in a small saucepan. Add the boiling water and place over medium heat. Bring to the boil, then simmer for 5 minutes until the glaze has reduced slightly and is syrupy. Strain, discarding the tea leaves, then set aside.

When the buns are cooked, remove them from the oven and brush liberally with the hot glaze. Let the buns cool slightly before serving with a big pot of something hot.

STORE & SHARE *These buns are at their best eaten warm from the oven on the day they are baked. Bundle up any extra buns and deliver them to a neighbour or store in an airtight container for a day or two. Be sure to reheat them gently before serving.*

When I was little, my mum used to make a pumpkin and prune cake. Naturally, as a kid it wasn't my favourite (not enough sprinkles), but happily, as an adult, the flavour combination has grown on me. These lovely, soft scones are a simple variation on that theme. Very easy to make – and eat – and, thanks to the pumpkin, a ridiculously cheerful yellow! Perfect breakfast or brunch fare, when something sweet, but not too sugary is in order.

Pumpkin & Prune Scones

MAKES 9 SCONES

275 g (9¾ oz) self-raising flour, plus extra to dust

⅛ teaspoon bicarbonate of soda (baking soda)

50 g (1¾ oz) unsalted butter, cold, cubed

¼ teaspoon fine sea salt

1 tablespoon caster (superfine) sugar

½ teaspoon ground mixed spice

80 g (2¾ oz) pitted prunes, roughly chopped

2 tablespoons (40 ml/1½ fl oz) full-cream (whole) milk

180 g (6½ oz) cooked pumpkin, mashed and cooled

1 egg, lightly beaten

1 tablespoon raw (demerara) sugar, to sprinkle

Salted butter, to serve

Preheat the oven to 190°C (375°F) fan-forced and line a baking tray with baking paper.

Place the flour and bicarbonate of soda in a large mixing bowl, mixing to combine. Scatter in the cold cubed butter and mix briefly, to coat all the pieces in flour. Then, using your fingertips, rub the butter into the flour until the mixture resembles coarse breadcrumbs. Stir in the salt, caster sugar and mixed spice along with the chopped prunes.

In a bowl, mix the milk into the mashed pumpkin, along with half of the egg (reserving the other half for glazing). Make a well in the centre of the dry ingredients and pour in the wet ingredients. Use a butter knife to gently mix the wet ingredients into the dry. When the dough starts to come together into a shaggy mass, use your hands to knead the dough briefly in the bowl until it comes together.

Tip the dough out onto a lightly floured surface and gently fold the dough a couple of times before shaping it into a rectangle about 3 cm (1¼ inches) in thickness. This is a soft, sticky dough, so use well-floured hands to shape it. Use a floured 5 cm (2 inch) round cutter to cut out as many scones as you can, making sure not to twist the cutter as you cut the scones. Gather up the offcuts and pat out again, cutting out the remaining scones. →

Nestle the scones close together on the prepared tray. Brush the tops with the reserved beaten egg and sprinkle with the raw sugar. Bake in the preheated oven for 15–18 minutes or until the tops are deep golden brown and the scones are cooked through. Allow the scones to cool for 10 minutes before serving them warm, split with lots of cold butter.

If you are not serving the scones straight away, wrap the hot scones in a clean tea towel (dish towel) to keep them warm until ready to serve.

STORE & SHARE *The scones are best eaten warm on the day they are made. Store any leftovers in an airtight container at room temperature to be eaten the next day, but please do reheat them before serving!*

When I was an exchange student in Germany, my favourite time of day was afternoon tea. My wonderful host-mother would visit the local bakery almost every day and return with the most delicious selection of baked goods. My favourite was always the streuselkuchen – a beautifully simple, yeasted dough topped with sweet crumble. Sometimes it had fruit nestled between the dough and rubbly streusel topping, and sometimes not. Either way, I loved it and those afternoon teas so much.

Adapted from my host-mother, Brigitte's, recipe, this is my take on those delicious streuselkuchens – soft, sweet, brioche-style dough topped with tart, cinnamony apples and a layer of brown-butter crumble. Sehr lecker!

Apple & Cinnamon Streuselkuchen

MAKES ONE 20 X 30CM SLICE (15 PIECES)

DOUGH
250 g (9 oz) bread flour
55 g (2 oz) caster (superfine)
   sugar
7 g (¼ oz) instant dried yeast
1 teaspoon vanilla bean paste
125 ml (4 fl oz) milk, just warm
60 g (2¼ oz) unsalted butter
½ teaspoon fine sea salt
1 egg, lightly beaten

BROWN BUTTER STREUSEL
   TOPPING
125 g (4½ oz) unsalted butter,
   cubed
200 g (7 oz) plain (all-purpose)
   flour
½ teaspoon ground cinnamon
⅛ teaspoon fine sea salt
110 g (3¾ oz) caster (superfine)
   sugar

Ingredients continued over page

First, start the dough by placing 50 g (1¾ oz) of the flour, 2 teaspoons of the sugar and the yeast in a medium mixing bowl. In a small jug, mix the vanilla into the just warm milk, then add 60 ml (2 fl oz) of this to the flour, sugar and yeast mixture. Stir to a smooth paste, cover and set aside for 45–60 minutes somewhere warm, until the mixture is bubbly and light. What we're doing here is a type of pre-ferment, which improves the flavour and texture of the cooked dough, making it softer and lighter. It also makes the dough less sticky and easier to work with when shaping. You can skip this step if you are short on time, but I think it's worth doing if you can.

Place the remaining milk and vanilla mixture along with the butter in a small saucepan and heat over low heat until the butter has melted. Remove from the heat and set aside to cool.

While the pre-ferment is bubbling and the milk is cooling, make the streusel topping. Brown the butter by placing it in a saucepan over medium heat. Cook the butter, swirling the pan occasionally, until the butter has melted and starts to bubble rapidly. Once the bubbles slow and the butter starts to foam, watch carefully. When small brown flecks appear at the bottom of the pan, quickly remove from the heat and set the butter aside to cool slightly. Place the flour, cinnamon, salt and sugar in a mixing bowl, whisking briefly to combine. Add the warm browned butter to the dry ingredients and mix to a soft crumble using a fork. Place the streusel in the fridge to chill until ready to use. →

CINNAMON APPLE FILLING

**6 eating apples, peeled, cored
and cut into 1 cm (½ inch)
pieces**

Juice of 1 lemon

1 teaspoon ground cinnamon

**55 g (2 oz) caster (superfine)
sugar**

When the pre-ferment is ready, place the remaining 200 g (7 oz) of bread flour, the remaining caster sugar and the salt in the bowl of a stand mixer with a dough hook. Add the just-warm milk mixture as well as the pre-ferment and egg, and mix on low speed until combined. Increase the speed to medium and continue to mix for 10–15 minutes, or until the dough is elastic and pulling away from the side of the bowl. This is a pretty soft dough so don't expect it to ball cleanly; rather you are looking for it to be stretchy and shiny and no longer stick to your fingers when pinched. Use buttered hands to transfer the dough to a well-buttered bowl and cover with plastic wrap. Place somewhere warm and allow to prove until doubled in size (1–2 hours).

While the dough is proving, make the apple filling by combining the diced apple, lemon juice, ground cinnamon and 80 ml (2½ fl oz) water in a medium saucepan. Mix well, cover with a lid and place over medium heat. Allow the mixture to come to the boil, before turning the heat down and allowing the fruit to bubble gently, stirring occasionally, for 10 minutes until soft. Add the sugar and continue to cook, with the lid off, for a couple of minutes, until most of the liquid has evaporated. Remove from the heat and set aside to cool.

When the dough has almost doubled in size, preheat the oven to 180°C (350°F) fan-forced and line the base and sides of a 20 x 30 cm (10 x 12 inch) slice (slab) or lamington tin with baking paper, leaving enough paper overhanging to help lift the cooked kuchen out of the tin.

When the dough has finished proving, gently press the air out of the dough and place it in the base of the prepared tin. Use your hands to stretch and spread the dough out into an even layer to cover the base of the tin. Use your fingertips to poke dimples in the surface of the dough, then top evenly with the cooled cinnamon apple mixture. Sprinkle over the streusel topping. Bake in the preheated oven for 25–35 minutes or until the dough is springy and cooked through, and the streusel topping is starting to brown.

Allow the streuselkuchen to cool in the tin for 15 minutes before carefully lifting it out onto a serving board and slicing. Serve warm with a pot of strong tea or cup of milky chai.

 STORE & SHARE *Store any leftovers in an airtight container in a cool place to eat the next day – just reheat gently before serving.*

It's a slippery slope, that first hot cross bun of the season – a steep descent towards carbohydrate-induced haze, but one I happily slide down (earlier, and earlier) each year! Now, I think my mum makes the best hot cross buns; I'm sure I am biased, but they really are good. She uses an old Nursing Mothers' Association recipe, which works every time. This is my adaptation of that recipe – updated to suit my tastes, using a combination of tart dried apricots, sultanas, currants and plenty of cinnamon. No mixed peel in sight!

   Like most yeasted bakes, this is not a recipe to make if you are in a hurry. This is a recipe to make when you have time; time to watch the mixer knead, time to watch the dough rise. Time to make pot after pot of tea and puddle around the kitchen, inhaling the heady scent of cooking buns.

Apricot & Sultana Hot Cross Buns

MAKES 16 BUNS

250 ml (9 fl oz) full-cream (whole) milk

2 teaspoons ground cinnamon

2 teaspoons ground mixed spice

1 teaspoon vanilla bean paste

2 teaspoons Earl Grey tea (or other black tea)

250 ml (9 fl oz) boiling water

150 g (5½ oz) dried apricots, roughly chopped

100 g (3½ oz) sultanas (golden raisins)

100 g (3½ oz) currants

500 g (1 lb 2 oz) bread flour

80 g (2¾ oz) caster (superfine) sugar

10 g (¼ oz) instant dried yeast

½ teaspoon fine sea salt

80 g (2¾ oz) unsalted butter, melted, plus extra to grease

1 egg, lightly beaten

Salted butter, to serve

Ingredients continued over page

First, place the milk, cinnamon, mixed spice and vanilla in a small saucepan. Place over low heat and bring to just below a simmer. Remove from the heat and set aside to cool until just warm.

   While the milk is cooling, brew the Earl Grey tea in the boiling water. Leave to steep for 3 minutes. Place the chopped apricots, along with the sultanas and currants in a mixing bowl. Strain the brewed tea and pour it over the dried fruit. Cover and leave to soak.

   When the spiced milk is just warm, start the dough by placing 100 g (3½ oz) of the bread flour, 1 tablespoon of the sugar and the yeast in a medium mixing bowl. Add 125 ml (4 fl oz) of the warm milk mixture to the bowl and stir to a smooth paste. Cover and set aside for 45–60 minutes somewhere warm, until the mixture is bubbly and light. What we're doing here is a type of pre-ferment, which improves the flavour and texture of the cooked dough, making it softer and lighter. It also makes the dough less sticky and easier to work with when shaping. You can skip this step if you are short on time, but I think it's worth doing if you can.

   When the pre-ferment is ready, place the remaining 400 g (14 oz) of bread flour, the remaining sugar and the salt in the bowl of a stand mixer with a dough hook. Add the remaining spiced milk, as well as the pre-ferment, the melted butter and egg, and mix on low speed until combined. Increase the speed to medium and continue to mix for 8–10 minutes until the dough is elastic and pulling away from the side of the bowl. →

FOR THE CROSSES

60 g (2¼ oz) plain (all-purpose)
   flour
1 teaspoon caster (superfine)
   sugar

GLAZE

2 tablespoons caster (superfine)
   sugar
½ teaspoon ground cinnamon
½ teaspoon gelatine powder

Drain the dried fruit well, reserving the tea soaking liquid for the glaze. Add the fruit to the dough and continue to mix for a further 5–8 minutes, until the fruit is well dispersed, and the dough is shiny and elastic. This is a pretty wet dough (which makes for a lovely light bun), so don't expect it to ball cleanly; rather you are looking for it to be stretchy and elastic, and to no longer stick to your fingers when pinched. Use buttered hands to transfer the dough to a well-buttered bowl and cover with plastic wrap. Place somewhere warm and allow to prove until doubled in size, 1–2 hours (or you can slow-prove the dough in the fridge overnight if you want to bake the buns the next morning).

When the dough has risen, grease one 32 cm (12¾ inch) round baking dish, or two 23 x 32 x 5 cm (9 x 12¾ x 2 inch) baking dishes, well with butter, or line with baking paper. Gently press the air out of the dough and divide into 16 evenly sized pieces. Roll each piece into a ball, tucking and folding the dough and pinching it together at the base. Place the balls close together in the greased baking dish/es. Cover lightly with plastic wrap, and allow to prove again somewhere warm for 30–60 minutes or until light and almost doubled in size.

While the buns are proving, preheat the oven to 180°C (350°F) fan-forced. In a small bowl, mix together the ingredients for the crosses. Add 50 ml (1½ fl oz) of cold water and mix to a smooth paste, adding a tiny bit more water if necessary, so that it is soft enough to pipe. Place the mixture in a small piping bag with a plain nozzle or use a small snaplock bag and snip a small hole in the end. Pipe crosses on the risen buns (or any other pattern that takes your fancy!).

Place the buns in the preheated oven to bake for 15 minutes. Turn the temperature down to 170°C (325°F) fan-forced and bake for a further 5–10 minutes for two rectangular dishes, or 10–15 minutes for one round dish, until the buns are golden brown and cooked through.

While the buns are cooking, place all the ingredients for the glaze in a small saucepan, along with 60 ml (2 fl oz) of the reserved tea. When the buns have 5 minutes left to bake, heat the glaze over low heat, stirring until the sugar and gelatine have dissolved. Let the glaze simmer over very low heat until the buns are cooked – watch the glaze carefully here, as it tends to boil over if it gets too hot.

When the buns are cooked, remove them from the oven and brush liberally with the hot glaze. Let the glaze soak in slightly before giving the buns another coat for glistening good measure!

STORE & SHARE *Share the buns warm from the oven (slathered in butter), with family and friends (but not my brother – he'll eat them all!), or split and toast them the next day. Best eaten within a day or two of baking.*

Here's to the little luxuries and edible cheer
that make life all the sweeter. To connection
and love, stuck together ever so eloquently
with sugar, butter and flour.

To the pantry keepers and postable love.
The biscuits we squirrel away, secretly, for a rainy day.
The bakes that are made with tenderness and care,
and posted to loved ones far away. The festive bakes
we share with greedy glee at celebrations, and the
ones we deliver with a hug and a kiss when words
fail to say how we feel. The little boxes of sunshine
left sitting on doorsteps, and the joy that comes from
sharing simple, home baking with family and friends.
This will never cease to delight me.

Pantry Keepers & Postable Love

I can never zest a lemon without then bringing it up to my nose for a deep inhale. There is something so deliciously fresh and energising about the scent of a just-zested lemon. All those little droplets of lemon oil fizzing in the air, ready to make your day just that little bit brighter. If I could bottle it, I think it might just be my signature scent. Sunshine in a bottle!

These little beauties – inspired by the large soft amaretti biscuits I can never help but buy at my local fruit shop – are a complete doddle to make. And I really do mean doddle; two bowls, no mixer, and a dose of sensory therapy thrown in for good measure. The addition of fennel seeds really does make these biscuits sing – so, even if you're not a particular fennel fan, do give these a go (at least once!).

Lemon & Fennel Seed Amaretti

MAKES ABOUT 18 BISCUITS * GLUTEN FREE

½ teaspoon fennel seeds

165 g (5¾ oz) caster (superfine) sugar

Finely grated zest of 2 lemons

200 g (7 oz) almond meal

3 tablespoons (40 g/1½ oz) slivered almonds

2 egg whites (approximately 70 g/2½ oz)

Pinch of fine sea salt

¼ teaspoon almond extract

50 g (1¾ oz) pure icing (confectioners') sugar, for rolling

Preheat the oven to 140°C (275°F) fan-forced and line a baking tray with baking paper.

Roughly crush the fennel seeds in a mortar and pestle, then place them in a mixing bowl along with the caster sugar and lemon zest. Use your fingertips to rub the zest and fennel seeds through the caster sugar (sensory play, wildly therapeutic!), until the sugar is fragrant and resembles damp sand. Add the almond meal and slivered almonds to the bowl and mix with a wooden spoon to combine.

Place the egg whites and salt in a mixing bowl and use a hand whisk to beat for a minute or two until frothy soft peaks form. Make a well in the centre of the dry ingredients and pour in the egg whites, along with the almond extract. Use a wooden spoon or spatula to mix thoroughly, until the dough comes together and is thick and sticky.

Scoop out scant tablespoons of dough and roll generously in icing sugar. Place on the baking tray, leaving a little room between the biscuits. Flatten the biscuits slightly with your fingertips then bake in the preheated oven for 18 minutes. Turn the oven off, leaving the biscuits in the oven to cool, with the door ajar.

When the biscuits are cool, serve with a cup of something hot.

STORE & SHARE *Amaretti keep happily in an airtight container at room temperature for up to 2 weeks. Or box them up carefully and send them off in the mail to a loved one! (See page 9 for tips on packing and posting baked goods.)*

I love apricots and gleefully look forward to them being in season each summer. But alas, the season is never long enough and, before I know it, they're gone again, despite my squirrel-like stockpiling efforts! But, luckily for me (and now you!), I have found a happy way to bridge the gap between seasons in the form of a very good dried apricot compote. It is tart, fruity and vibrant – and particularly good sandwiched between two layers of buttery cardamom-scented shortbread, as you find here. The key to making the finest apricot compote is starting with good-quality dried fruit. Use the best local, sun-dried, tart apricots you can find.

This recipe also works beautifully with 300 g (10½ oz) Good Fruit Mince (page 217) sandwiched between the shortbread, in place of the apricot compote, for a delightful festive spin.

Apricot Shortbread Slice

MAKES ONE 20 CM (8 INCH) SQUARE SLICE (12 PIECES)

DRIED APRICOT COMPOTE
200 g (7 oz) dried apricots,
　roughly chopped
55 g (2 oz) caster (superfine)
　sugar
1 teaspoon vanilla bean paste
Juice of 1 lemon

SHORTBREAD
110 g (3¾ oz) caster (superfine)
　sugar, plus 1 tablespoon extra
　to sprinkle
Finely grated zest of 1 lemon
225 g (8 oz) unsalted butter,
　softened
2 teaspoons vanilla bean paste
200 g (7 oz) plain (all-purpose)
　flour
100 g (3½ oz) white rice flour
⅛ teaspoon fine sea salt
½ teaspoon ground cardamom

Line the base and sides of a 20 cm (8 inch) square cake tin with baking paper, leaving enough paper overhanging to help lift the cooked slice out of the tin.

First, make the dried apricot compote by combining the apricots, sugar, vanilla, lemon juice and 150 ml (5 fl oz) water in a medium saucepan. Stir and place, covered, over low heat. Bring the mixture to a simmer, then allow to cook, stirring occasionally with the lid askew, for 10–12 minutes or until the apricots are soft and collapsing, and almost all the liquid has been absorbed. Remove from the heat and allow to cool.

While the compote is cooling, preheat the oven to 150°C (300°F) fan-forced.

When the compote is cool, make the shortbread by placing the sugar and lemon zest in the bowl of a stand mixer with a paddle attachment. Mix on low for a minute or so to allow the zest to flavour the sugar, before adding the softened butter and vanilla. Beat on medium speed until light and fluffy.

Place the plain flour, rice flour, salt and cardamom in a separate bowl, and use a hand whisk to briefly combine. Add the dry ingredients to the creamed butter and sugar mixture, mixing until a soft dough comes together. Divide the dough in half and use your clean hands, or an offset palette knife, to gently press one half of the shortbread dough out into a thin, even layer in the base of your tin. →

Spread the cooled apricot compote evenly over the shortbread base. Pinch off walnut-sized pieces of the remaining shortbread dough, flatten with your fingers, and place on top of the apricot compote. Use your fingers to squash and spread the shortbread out into an even-ish layer to cover the compote.

Sprinkle the top with the extra caster sugar, then bake in the preheated oven for 45–55 minutes, or until the shortbread is cooked and is starting to colour. The shortbread will still be a bit soft at this stage, but will firm up as it cools. Allow the slice to cool completely in the tin before using the extra baking paper to lift it out. Slice into bars with a sharp knife and serve with a large pot of tea. Earl Grey is an especially nice combination here.

STORE & SHARE *Store any leftovers in an airtight container in a cool place for up to a week. This slice is sturdy enough to be snugly packed in a box and posted too – just make sure to send it express post so the recipient has time to enjoy it! (See page 9 for tips on packing and posting baked goods.)*

Now, these biscuits are definitely one for the tastes-better-than-it-looks club, but don't let that put you off. What they lack in aesthetic appeal, they more than make up for in flavour! Crunchy, deeply chocolatey and crisp, with little nuggets of golden crystalised ginger and milk chocolate, they are immensely satisfying with a cup of tea or a small strong coffee. A word of warning though, once you start eating them, it is rather hard to stop!

These biscotti keep really well too, making them ideal to make and gift, or even send off in the post for a little edible cheer to a loved one far away. (See page 9 for tips on packing and posting baked goods.)

Double Chocolate & Ginger Biscotti

MAKES ABOUT 40 BISCUITS

110 g (3¾ oz) caster (superfine) sugar
130 g (4½ oz) light brown sugar
1 teaspoon vanilla bean paste
2 eggs
300 g (10½ oz) self-raising flour
40 g (1½ oz) Dutch-process (unsweetened) cocoa powder, sifted
¼ teaspoon fine sea salt
150 g (5½ oz) milk chocolate, roughly chopped
80 g (2¾ oz) crystallised ginger, cut into 1 cm (½ inch) pieces
80 g (2¾ oz) unsalted butter, melted and cooled

Place the caster sugar, brown sugar, vanilla and eggs in the bowl of a stand mixer with a whisk attachment and whisk, scraping down the side of the bowl once or twice, until the mixture is thick and pale, 2–3 minutes.

Place the flour, cocoa, salt, chocolate and ginger in a separate bowl and mix to combine. Add the dry ingredients and the cooled melted butter to the whisked egg mixture and mix until a soft, sticky dough forms. Set the dough aside, covered in the bowl, somewhere cool for 15–30 minutes (in the fridge if the weather is hot) to firm up a little.

While the dough is resting, preheat the oven to 170°C (325°F) fan-forced and line two baking trays with baking paper. When rested, divide the mixture in two and roll each portion into a log about 22 cm (8½ inches) long.

Place the dough logs on the baking trays (one per tray). Bake in the preheated oven for 25 minutes, or until the surface of the logs is crackled and set. They will still be soft inside, but this is as it should be. Remove the trays from the oven and allow the biscuit logs to cool on the trays for 20 minutes. Lower the oven temperature to 150°C (300°F) fan-forced.

Use a large, serrated knife to cut the logs into 1 cm (½ inch) thick slices. Gently hold and squeeze the sides of the logs together as you cut, as the dough will be quite soft and crumbly at this point. Don't worry if some of the edges crumble off as you are slicing, this to be expected, and we are going for rustically delicious, not perfect! →

Use a palette knife to carefully place the sliced biscotti back on the trays and return to the oven for 15–18 minutes, turning them over after about 10 minutes, until the surface of the biscuits is dry. Let the biscotti cool completely on the trays before serving or storing.

STORE & SHARE *The biscotti keep well in an airtight container at room temperature for up to 2 weeks. Well wrapped and packed in a bubble wrap–lined box these also make a very happy postable treat!*

When I worked at a tea shop, we sold beautifully packaged tea-infused biscuits. My favourites were always the Earl Grey ones. We used to put them out for tastings each morning, and I think I was solely responsible for their consumption most days! These little rounds, fragrant with ground Earl Grey and orange zest, make an excellent tea biscuit. Polenta gives them a pleasant chew and, accompanying a cup of hot tea, they are rather hard to resist. These keep remarkably well, so save a jar, squirrelled away in the pantry, for tea-related emergencies. Or wrap well and post to a friend in need of a biscuity hello! (See page 9 for tips on packing and posting baked goods.)

Earl Grey & Polenta Rounds

MAKES ABOUT 40 BISCUITS

2 teaspoons loose-leaf Earl Grey tea

110 g (3¾ oz) caster (superfine) sugar

Finely grated zest of 1 orange

200 g (7 oz) unsalted butter, softened

1 teaspoon vanilla bean paste

200 g (7 oz) plain (all-purpose) flour, plus extra to dust

¼ teaspoon baking powder

100 g (3½ oz) fine (instant) polenta

¼ teaspoon of fine sea salt

Place the Earl Grey tea in a small spice grinder or mortar and pestle and grind until fine. Place in the bowl of a stand mixer along with the sugar and orange zest and use your fingertips to rub the zest and tea through the sugar until fragrant. Add the butter and vanilla and, using the paddle attachment, beat until light and fluffy.

Place the flour, baking powder, polenta and salt in a separate bowl and use a hand whisk to combine. Add the dry ingredients to the creamed butter mixture, mixing gently until the dough just comes together. Tip the mixture out onto a lightly floured surface and use your hands to bring the dough together into a ball.

Roll the dough out between two sheets of baking paper until it is about 5 mm (¼ inch) thick. Place in the fridge for an hour or so until firm enough to cut. While the dough is chilling, preheat the oven to 140°C (275°F) fan-forced and line two baking trays with baking paper.

When the dough is ready, use a 5 cm (2 inch) round cutter to cut out the biscuits, re-rolling the dough as necessary. Place the biscuits on the prepared trays, leaving a little space in-between as they will spread while cooking.

Bake in the preheated oven for 18–22 minutes or until the biscuits are just starting to colour. Remove from the oven, then allow the biscuits to cool completely on the trays. Serve in generous quantities with a big pot of tea.

STORE & SHARE *Store for up to a month in an airtight container.*

This is a 'recipe' in a very loose sense of the word – it's really just a collection of delicious things bathed in chocolate. But with tart sour cherries, roasted pistachios and glorious pink rose Turkish delight, what could go wrong? A word of warning: cut it into small pieces, as it is rather sweet.

I must admit something here, though. Every time I make this and find myself sprinkling the top liberally with rose petals, I am reminded of the infamous gift-wrapping scene from the movie *Love Actually*. I resisted the urge to dip it in yoghurt and cover it in chocolate buttons. But only just! I also think I may have watched that movie a few too many times ...?

Sour Cherry, Pistachio & Rose Rocky Road

MAKES ONE 20 CM (8 INCH) SQUARE SLICE (18 PIECES) * GLUTEN FREE

200 g (7 oz) dark chocolate (45–55% cocoa solids), roughly chopped

200 g (7 oz) gluten-free milk chocolate, roughly chopped

80 g (2¾ oz) dried sour cherries

100 g (3½ oz) roasted pistachios (see page 9)

100 g (3½ oz) gluten-free marshmallows, cut in half

200 g (7 oz) rose-flavoured Turkish delight, roughly chopped

45 g (1½ oz) freeze-dried strawberries, roughly chopped

Sprinkle of flaky sea salt

1 tablespoon dried edible rose petals (optional)

Line a 20 cm (8 inch) square cake tin with baking paper, leaving enough paper overhanging to help lift the rocky road out of the tin when set.

First, place the dark and milk chocolate in a heatproof bowl set over a saucepan of gently simmering water, making sure that the water doesn't touch the base of the bowl. Allow the chocolate to melt, stirring now and then, until you have a gloriously smooth chocolate puddle. Remove the bowl from the heat and allow it to cool slightly.

Place the sour cherries, pistachios and halved marshmallows in a separate large bowl, tossing to combine. Reserve a few pieces of Turkish delight and a little of the freeze-dried strawberry to decorate the top of the rocky road, then mix the rest in with the sour cherry and pistachio mixture. Pour the slightly cooled melted chocolate over the top, then add a generous smattering of the flaky sea salt. Stir gently, but thoroughly, until all the ingredients are bathed in chocolate.

Spoon the mixture into the prepared tin, gently squashing it down with the back of a spoon. Scatter the reserved Turkish delight and freeze-dried strawberries over the top, along with the dried rose petals (if using). Refrigerate, uncovered, until set (a good couple of hours).

Slice into pieces using a large sharp knife and serve with tea or coffee.

STORE & SHARE *I like to wrap individual slices of rocky road in cellophane and tie with ribbon to give as gifts. Rocky road will keep in an airtight container somewhere cool (in the fridge if the weather is warm) for up to 2 weeks.*

For me, these biscuits are a double dose of festive cheer. I can remember when I was a child, my parents sometimes buying a box of almond crescent biscuits at Christmas time – the kind where each time you opened the tin you were met with a cloud of sweet icing sugar. I loved those biscuits as a kid, and I still love them now. They are imbued with the delicious joy of childhood and the nostalgia of Christmases past. (That's a lot of pressure on a small biscuit!) My version comes with the added merriment of chai tea which, heavily spiced as it is, always seems particularly festive. Don't skimp on the icing sugar dusting – the biscuits should look as though they've just emerged from a snowstorm!

Chai & Almond Crescents

MAKES ABOUT 20 BISCUITS

2 teaspoons loose-leaf chai tea

80 g (2¾ oz) almonds (skin on)

125 g (4½ oz) unsalted butter, softened

60 g (2¼ oz) icing (confectioners') sugar mixture, plus extra to dust

1 teaspoon vanilla bean paste

100 g (3½ oz) plain (all-purpose) flour

50 g (1¾ oz) cornflour (cornstarch)

¼ teaspoon fine sea salt

¼ teaspoon ground cardamom

¼ teaspoon ground cinnamon

Place the chai tea and almonds in a small food processor and blitz until fine. Set aside.

Place the butter, sugar and vanilla in the bowl of a stand mixer with a paddle attachment and beat until light. Place the plain flour, cornflour, ground almond mixture, salt and spices in a separate bowl and use a hand whisk to combine. Add the dry ingredients to the creamed butter mixture and stir briefly to form a soft dough. Let the dough rest, covered, in the bowl somewhere cool for 20–30 minutes. This allows the dough to firm up a little, making it easier to roll.

While the dough is resting, preheat the oven to 150°C (300°F) fan-forced and line two baking trays with baking paper.

When ready to bake, pinch off scant tablespoons of dough and use your hands to roll them into little 8 cm (3¼ inch) long logs. Shape into crescents and place on the prepared trays, leaving space between the biscuits as they will spread while cooking.

Bake in the preheated oven for 14–18 minutes, or until the biscuits are just starting to colour. Allow to cool on the trays for 5 minutes before dusting generously with the extra icing sugar. Let the biscuits cool completely on the trays before serving or storing.

STORE & SHARE *The biscuits will keep happily in an airtight container at room temperature for up to a month, and will post well too, making an excellent addition to a Christmas gift box. (See page 9 for tips on packing and posting baked goods.)*

Some days require a little sugar coating. This is a recipe for those days. The ones where your to-do list feels endless, the house is a mess, or the air just feels a little too heavy. It is chock-full of sweet, smile-inducing things: caramelly brown sugar and browned butter, malted milk powder, chocolate and hazelnuts. Just the action of making it helps me to feel a little more cheerful, hopeful and hungry. It also travels remarkably well to a picnic, to a barbecue, or well-wrapped and boxed, in the post. Portable joy. Maybe blondes do have more fun?

Malted Hazelnut Blondies

MAKES ONE 20 CM (8 INCH) SQUARE SLICE (16 PIECES)

200 g (7 oz) unsalted butter, cubed

110 g (3¾ oz) golden (raw) caster (superfine) sugar

110 g (3¾ oz) light brown sugar

1 teaspoon vanilla bean paste

3 eggs

150 g (5½ oz) plain (all-purpose) flour

¼ teaspoon fine sea salt

3 tablespoons (30 g/1 oz) malted milk powder

100 g (3½ oz) white chocolate, roughly chopped

100 g (3½ oz) store-bought chocolate hazelnut spread

50 g (1¾ oz) hazelnuts, halved

Flaky sea salt, to sprinkle

Preheat the oven to 160°C (325°F) fan-forced. Line the base and sides of a 20 cm (8 inch) square cake tin with baking paper, leaving enough paper overhanging to help lift the cooked blondie out of the tin.

First, brown the butter by placing it in a saucepan over medium heat. Cook the butter, swirling the pan occasionally, until the butter has melted and starts to bubble rapidly. Once the bubbles slow and the butter starts to foam, watch carefully. When small brown flecks appear at the bottom of the pan, quickly remove from the heat and set the butter aside to cool slightly.

When the browned butter has cooled to warm, place the caster sugar, brown sugar, vanilla and eggs in a large mixing bowl and use a hand whisk to mix well. Whisk in the warm browned butter.

In a separate bowl, place the flour, salt and malted milk powder, mixing to combine. Fold the dry ingredients, along with half the chopped white chocolate, into the egg and sugar mixture. Pour the batter into the prepared tin, smoothing the top with a spatula. Gently dot the top of the blondie with the remaining white chocolate, spoonfuls of the chocolate hazelnut spread, and the chopped hazelnuts.

Sprinkle the surface with flaky sea salt and bake in the preheated oven for 25–35 minutes or until the surface of the blondie is set, but it is still a little wobbly in the middle. The blondie will continue to cook as it cools, and you want it to be a little soft inside. →

Allow to cool completely in the tin before carefully lifting the blondie out and slicing. Serve at room temperature or warmed a little, with a bottomless pot of tea.

STORE & SHARE *Store any leftovers in an airtight container in a cool place for up to a week, or package up and post to a friend in need of sugar! (See page 9 for tips on packing and posting baked goods.)*

I was first introduced to these festive biscuits as a teenager by my lovely host-family, when I was an exchange student in Germany. I had never had anything like them before – chewy, nutty and sweet, with a snowy layer of crisp meringue icing. They fell out of my life for the next decade or so, until I was again reminded of how wonderful they were by their appearance in a Christmas parcel from Germany. They made it all the way to Australia in one piece and were, I think, all the more delicious for it! Since then, they have been on our annual Christmas bake-list.

I've taken the liberty of adding maple syrup and freshly grated nutmeg to my biscuits – giving them an added caramelly sweetness, not to mention adorable nutmeg freckles on their dusky meringue tops. Someone pass me the fairy lights!

Cinnamon Maple Stars

MAKES ABOUT 36 BISCUITS * GLUTEN FREE

2 egg whites (approximately 70 g/2½ oz)

⅛ teaspoon fine sea salt

200 g (7 oz) pure icing (confectioners') sugar, sifted

320 g (11¼ oz) almond meal

3 teaspoons ground cinnamon

¼ teaspoon freshly ground nutmeg, plus extra to top

2 tablespoons maple syrup

Preheat the oven to 120°C (250°F) fan-forced and line three baking trays with baking paper.

Place the egg whites and salt in the bowl of a stand mixer with a whisk attachment and whisk until soft peaks form. Add the sugar, a few tablespoons at a time, and continue to whisk until all the sugar is incorporated and the meringue is thick and glossy. Place 80 g (2¾ oz) of the meringue mixture in a separate small bowl and set aside for icing the biscuits.

Place the almond meal, cinnamon and nutmeg in a separate bowl and use a hand whisk to combine. Add the dry ingredients to the mixer bowl containing the remainder of the meringue, along with 1½ tablespoons of the maple syrup. Use a wooden spoon or spatula to mix thoroughly to a thick, sticky dough.

Roll the dough out between two sheets of baking paper until it is 5 mm (¼ inch) thick. Use a 6 cm (2½ inch) star-shaped biscuit cutter to cut out as many biscuits as you can, placing them spaced out a little on the prepared baking trays as they will spread while cooking. As this is a soft, sticky dough, take your time and handle the biscuits gently when transferring them to the trays. You may need to wash your biscuit cutter halfway through, or dust it with icing sugar as you go, as the dough tends to stick, making it hard to remove the biscuits in one piece. If you find the dough too soft to work with, pop the rolled-out dough in the fridge for 30 minutes before cutting the biscuits out. Gather up the dough offcuts and roll them out again, cutting out the remaining biscuits. →

Add the remaining maple syrup to the reserved meringue mixture to loosen it slightly and mix until smooth. Top the biscuits with a small spoonful of the meringue and use the back of a teaspoon, or a butter knife, to spread the meringue out into a thin layer over the surface of the biscuits, pulling it right out to the points of the stars. Grate a little extra nutmeg over the tops.

Bake in the preheated oven for 18–20 minutes or until the meringue topping is crisp and is a light, dusky beige. The biscuits will still be soft underneath, but they will firm up a little as they cool. They should still have a little chew to them when cooled. Allow the biscuits to cool completely on the trays before moving them; if you try and move them while they are still hot you may tear the soft bottoms off.

STORE & SHARE *The cinnamon stars will keep happily in an airtight container at room temperature for up to 3 weeks. They make an excellent festive gift and can also be bundled up in a well-padded box and posted. (See page 9 for tips on packing and posting baked goods.)*

To me, the lead-up to Christmas never feels quite right until a batch or two of gingerbread has been made. One to be made and decorated, noisily and with many sprinkles, by the kids (I think of this as the maximalist batch); and another made quietly, in secret, by myself and decorated sparingly to satisfy my delicate aesthetic sensibilities (the minimalist batch)! Needless to say, everyone always loves the bright, garishly-garnished kids' batch best! We make our biscuits lightly spiced, without too much heat, as my daughter is not a ginger fan. But feel free to up the ginger if that's your thing!

Gently Spiced Gingerbread

MAKES 25–30 ICED BISCUITS

BISCUITS

125 g (4½ oz) unsalted butter, softened

75 g (2½ oz) light brown sugar

75 g (2½ oz) caster (superfine) sugar

1 tablespoon (30 g/1 oz) golden syrup (light treacle)

1 teaspoon vanilla bean paste

1 egg, lightly beaten

250 g (9 oz) plain (all-purpose) flour, plus extra to dust

¼ teaspoon bicarbonate of soda (baking soda)

¼ teaspoon fine sea salt

2 teaspoons ground ginger

1 teaspoon ground mixed spice

Ingredients continued over page

To make the biscuits, place the butter, brown sugar, caster sugar, golden syrup and vanilla in the bowl of a stand mixer with a paddle attachment and beat until light. Add the egg and beat again until smooth.

Place the flour, bicarbonate of soda, salt and spices in a separate bowl and use a hand whisk to combine. Add the dry ingredients to the creamed butter mixture and mix until a soft dough forms. Use a rolling pin to roll the dough out between two sheets of well-floured baking paper until it is about 5 mm (¼ inch) thick. Place in the fridge for 30–60 minutes, or until firm enough to cut out.

While the dough is chilling, preheat the oven to 150°C (300°F) fan-forced and line three baking trays with baking paper.

Remove the dough from the fridge, take off the top layer of baking paper and use biscuit cutters to cut the dough into your desired shapes, re-rolling offcuts as necessary (and popping the dough back in the fridge if it softens up too much). Place the biscuits on the prepared trays, leaving a little space between each as they will spread while cooking.

Bake the biscuits in the preheated oven for 10–12 minutes or until they are golden brown and smell deliciously toasty. Allow to cool on the trays for 5 minutes before carefully transferring to a wire rack to cool completely. →

**GENTLY SPICED
GINGERBREAD CONTINUED**

ICING (FROSTING)
1 egg white
**250 g (9 oz) pure icing
(confectioners') sugar, sifted**
⅛ teaspoon ground cardamom
2 teaspoons orange juice
Sprinkles to decorate (optional)

When the biscuits are cool, make the icing by whisking the egg white in a medium mixing bowl until frothy. Add 200 g (7 oz) of the icing sugar and the cardamom and mix until smooth, before stirring in the orange juice. Divide the mixture evenly between two bowls. Cover one bowl and set aside – this is your glaze icing. Add the remaining 50 g (1¾ oz) of icing sugar to the other bowl and mix until smooth. Check that it is a good, thick consistency to pipe (adding a little more icing sugar or a drop more orange juice if required). Spoon into a piping bag with a small plain nozzle (a plastic snaplock bag with the end snipped off works too) and secure the end.

Pipe outlines around the edges of the biscuits and allow them to set before spooning on a little glaze icing and using the back of a spoon to spread it out, filling in the piped outline. Decorate with sprinkles (if using), and allow the icing to set before serving or storing.

STORE & SHARE *The un-iced biscuits will keep happily in an airtight container at room temperature for up to a month. Iced biscuits keep well for up to 2 weeks. They also make wonderful gifts – just bundle them up in some cellophane and tie with a ribbon – and are sturdy enough to be posted. (See page 9 for tips on packing and posting baked goods.)*

Trays of fragrant, syrupy baked fruit and jars of jewel-coloured jam. Seasons and sentiment preserved with patience and care. Softly collapsing stone fruit and the perfume of baked autumn quince. This is the fruit I love to cook and eat; often straight from the tray, sweet pink juice running all down my arms.

There should be a special word for the type of joy one experiences at the sight of an unopened jar of homemade jam; because there is nothing more life-affirming on a dreary day than a slice of good toast or a fluffy, warm scone with a thick layer of butter and a dollop of excellent jam. Except, maybe, for a tray of gloriously soft, sweetly baked fruit; peaches and plums, baked until tender and fragrant. Heat and sugar turn even the most unpromising specimens into puddles of heaven.

Puddles of Jam & Sweet Baked Fruit

Apricots are one of my all-time favourites – and as one of the last few truly seasonal fruits, I find it necessary to preserve them every year, in jam form, to enjoy on toast and to use in bakes throughout the year.

I make this simple jam, along with the Plum & Star Anise and Strawberry & Rhubarb jams that follow, in a baking tray in the oven, as I find it much easier than traditional jam-making. The result is a lovely soft-set, intensely fruity jam. You will need five 250 ml (9 fl oz) sterilised jars (see page 9), or equivalent, to store the jam. It is important to note that as my jam recipes have a lower sugar to fruit ratio than traditional jams, the shelf life will be shorter, but the flavour so much more vibrant – this is a trade-off I'm willing to make!

Roast Apricot Jam

MAKES APPROXIMATELY 1.5 KG (3 LB 5 OZ) JAM

1.5 kg (3 lb 5 oz) apricots

750 g (1 lb 10 oz) caster (superfine) sugar

80 ml (2½ fl oz) lemon juice (about 2–3 lemons)

1 vanilla bean, split and seeds scraped, or 1 tablespoon vanilla bean paste

Preheat the oven to 180°C (350°F) fan-forced. Wash the apricots and cut them in half, discarding the pits. Cut each half in half again and place in a large, deep baking tray. Add the sugar, lemon juice, vanilla bean and seeds (or paste), along with 60 ml (2 fl oz) of water and mix well.

Spread the apricot pieces out into an even layer and place the tray in the preheated oven to cook for 25 minutes, or until the mixture is bubbling around the edges. Carefully take the tray out of the oven and gently mash the apricots with a fork or potato masher.

Return the tray to the oven and cook for a further 15 minutes, before carefully stirring and mashing the mixture again. Return the jam to the oven for a final 10–15 minutes, or until the jam is thick, fragrant and bubbling. Watch the jam carefully during the final two stints in the oven, as it tends to bubble over if it gets too hot. Open the oven door and give the jam a little stir if it's looking like it might bubble over, or take the tray out of the oven a few minutes early if it looks like it is ready. When the jam is cooked, carefully remove the tray from the oven and give it a final little mash with a fork. Ladle the jam into sterilised jars and seal while hot.

STORE & SHARE *Unopened jam will keep for up to 3 months in a cool place. Once opened, store in the refrigerator and use within a month. This jam also makes a wonderful gift – if you can bear to part with it!*

(Pictured on page 208)

Sweet and tart and with just a hint of warm spice, this beautiful jewel-bright jam is one of my favourites. You will need four 250 ml (9 fl oz) sterilised jars (see page 9), or equivalent, to store the jam. Make sure to remove any star anise pieces before you use this jam in any bakes; otherwise they do rather get stuck in your teeth!

Plum & Star Anise Jam

MAKES APPROXIMATELY 1.3 KG (3 LB) JAM

1 kg (2 lb 3 oz) plums (I like
    to use small red plums)
650 g (1 lb 7 oz) caster
    (superfine) sugar
125 ml (4 fl oz) lemon juice
    (about 3–4 lemons)
1 vanilla bean, split and seeds
    scraped, or 1 tablespoon
    vanilla bean paste
4 star anise

Preheat the oven to 180°C (350°F) fan-forced. Wash the plums and cut them into quarters, discarding the pits. Place the plum quarters in a large, deep baking tray and add the sugar, lemon juice, vanilla bean and seeds (or paste) and star anise. Mix well, then spread the plums out in an even layer. Place the tray in the preheated oven to cook for 25 minutes, stirring once or twice, until the mixture is bubbling around the edges. Carefully take the tray out of the oven and gently mash the plums with a fork or potato masher.

Return the tray to the oven and cook for a further 20–25 minutes, carefully stirring the mixture once or twice during the cooking time, until thick and bubbling. Watch the jam carefully when nearing the end of the cooking time, as it can bubble over if it gets too hot. Open the oven door and give the jam a little stir if it's looking like it might bubble over, or take the tray out of the oven a few minutes early if it is nicely thickened.

When the jam is cooked, carefully remove the tray from the oven. Give the fruit another mash, then ladle into sterilised jars and seal while hot.

STORE & SHARE *Unopened jam will keep for up to 3 months in a cool place. Once opened, store in the refrigerator and use within a month. Make sure to remove any star anise pieces before using the jam in any recipes.*

(Pictured on page 209)

From left to right: Roast Apricot Jam (page 206), Strawberry & Rhubarb Jam (page 211), Passionfruit Curd (page 210), Plum & Star Anise Jam (page 207).

Spreadable, edible sunshine! It's impossible not to feel just a little more optimistic in the face of a jar of this sunny-yellow passionfruit curd. Use it to top scones, fill cakes, or fold through whipped cream or buttercream. Or just eat it with a spoon straight from the jar.

Passionfruit Curd

MAKES APPROXIMATELY 300 g (10½ oz) CURD

80 ml (2½ fl oz) fresh
  passionfruit pulp (from about
  3–4 passionfruit)
Finely grated zest of 1 lemon
2 tablespoons lemon juice
110 g (3¾ oz) caster (superfine)
  sugar
1 whole egg, plus 1 egg yolk
Pinch of fine sea salt
60 g (2¼ oz) unsalted butter,
  cubed

Place all the ingredients, except the butter, in a medium stainless steel bowl, taking care not to let the egg yolks sit around on the sugar for too long. Whisk well to combine, then add the cubed butter. Set the bowl over a saucepan of gently simmering water, making sure the water does not touch the base of the bowl. Heat the mixture, stirring with a rubber spatula or whisk until the sugar has dissolved and the butter has melted.

Continue to cook the curd, stirring continually, for 5–7 minutes or until slightly thickened. Take care not to let the mixture get too hot or you will risk scrambling the eggs! Transfer the curd to a heatproof bowl or sterilised jar (see page 9) and seal – or cover the surface directly with plastic wrap. Allow to cool slightly, then refrigerate until cold before using.

STORE & SHARE *Store the curd in the fridge and use within a week. A jar of sunny curd, along with a batch of fresh Sugared Buttermilk & Lemon Scones (page 161) wrapped in a tea towel (dish towel) also happen to make the most wonderful doorstep delivery!*

(Pictured on page 209)

Strawberry and rhubarb jam has long been a favourite of mine. My mum makes a delicious version, and has done for as long as I can remember. This is perhaps owing to the excellent rhubarb that my dad grows, which lately has outdone itself in height, quantity and ruby-red colour. I have major rhubarb envy.

You will need one large (750 ml/26 fl oz) sterilised jar (see page 9) for the jam or, if you plan to use it straightaway, you can simply decant the jam into a clean container and store in the fridge.

Strawberry & Rhubarb Jam

MAKES APPROXIMATELY 1 KG (2 LB 3 OZ) JAM

500 g (1 lb 2 oz) strawberries, hulled and quartered

300 g (10½ oz) rhubarb, cut into 2 cm (¾ inch) pieces

440 g (14 oz) caster (superfine) sugar

125 ml (4 fl oz) lemon juice (about 3–4 lemons)

1 vanilla bean, split and seeds scraped or 1 tablespoon vanilla bean paste

2 teaspoons rosewater (optional)

Preheat the oven to 180°C (350°F) fan-forced. Place the strawberries, rhubarb, sugar, lemon juice and vanilla bean seeds and pod (or paste) in a large deep baking tray and mix well, making sure that no dry bits of sugar remain.

Spread the fruit out into an even layer and place the tray in the preheated oven to cook for 20 minutes, or until the fruit is bubbling around the edges of the tray. Carefully take the tray out of the oven and mash the fruit with a potato masher or fork.

Return the tray to the oven and cook for a further 15–20 minutes. Watch the jam carefully at this point as it can bubble over if it is cooked for too long. When the jam has reduced slightly and is bubbling and fragrant, carefully remove the tray from the oven. Give the jam another little mash, stir in the rosewater (if using), then ladle it into a sterilised jar and seal while hot.

STORE & SHARE *Unopened jam will keep for up to 3 months in a cool place. Once opened, store in the refrigerator and use within a month.*

(Pictured on page 208)

This is the softly collapsing, jammy fruit of my dreams. Tart and sweet at the same time, thanks to the lemon juice and sugar, this is how I like my fruit. I could (and regularly do) eat it just as it is, with a spoonful of yoghurt or vanilla ice cream. But it is also exceptionally good buried in the base of a tart, or crowning a little custard number. I often make a double batch when peaches or plums are in season, so as to have enough to bake with and also to eat straight from the tray.

Baked Stone Fruit

MAKES ONE MEDIUM TRAY

6 plums or small ripe peaches

2 tablespoons caster (superfine) sugar

Juice of 1 lemon

½ teaspoon vanilla bean paste

1 teaspoon rosewater

Preheat the oven to 190°C (375°F) fan-forced and line a medium baking dish with baking paper.

Wash the plums or peaches and cut them in half, discarding the pits. Place the halves, cut side up, in the baking dish and sprinkle with sugar. Squeeze the lemon juice over and drizzle with the vanilla.

Bake in the preheated oven for 20 minutes. Take the tray out of the oven and carefully turn the fruit over, so the skin side is facing up, then return to the oven for a further 5–10 minutes, or until the fruit is soft, but still holding its shape. Sprinkle with the rosewater and allow to cool in the tray before using your fingers to gently slip the skins from the fruit. Discard the skins. Place the fruit in a container in a single layer and pour any of the pan juices over the top. Cover and store in the fridge until ready to use.

 STORE & SHARE *The baked stone fruit keeps well in an airtight container in the fridge for 3–4 days.*

(Pictured on page 214)

Rhubarb is a firm favourite in our family, and has been for as long as I can remember. This lovely marmalade baked rhubarb is a variation on a recipe I shared in my first book, *The Plain Cake Appreciation Society*, and, quite frankly, I love it. The subtle citrus flavour and mild bitterness of the marmalade work beautifully paired with the glorious pink-fruitiness of the soft baked rhubarb. Serve it with custard or ice cream for a simple dessert, use it in my Little Pound Cakes (page 125), or as an alternative to quince in my Quince & Ricotta Crumble Squares (page 35). Save the syrup from the pan too – top it up with bubbly water for a delicious fruity cordial, or add it to Prosecco for a cheeky pink drink!

Marmalade Baked Rhubarb

MAKES 350 g (12 OZ) BAKED RHUBARB

350 g (12 oz) rhubarb, cut into
  5 cm (2 inch) lengths
3 tablespoons caster (superfine)
  sugar
Juice of 1 orange, plus 3 thick
  strips of zest
1 teaspoon vanilla bean paste
2 tablespoons orange
  marmalade

Preheat the oven to 180°C (350°F) fan-forced and place the rhubarb, sugar, orange juice, zest and vanilla in a medium baking dish and toss to combine. Arrange the rhubarb in a single layer and bake in the preheated oven for 10 minutes.

Remove the rhubarb from the oven and spoon the marmalade over the top. Gently turn the fruit over to coat it in the marmalade and syrup and return the tray to the oven for 5–10 minutes, or until the rhubarb is tender but still holds its shape. Allow to cool in the tray.

 STORE & SHARE *Store the baked rhubarb and syrup in an airtight container in the fridge and eat within 3–4 days.*

(Pictured on page 214)

Top: Baked Stone Fruit (page 212). Bottom: Marmalade Baked Rhubarb (page 213).

From left to right: Baked Quince (page 216), Good Fruit Mince (page 217).

Baked quince is, in my opinion, one of life's real pleasures. It is not an easy win, by any means, but somehow the labour involved makes it all the more rewarding (not to mention delicious). The transformation quince undergoes, from hard, mealy and frankly unpromising, to soft, fragrant crimson flesh is nothing short of miraculous. The key word here is patience.

This recipe makes enough for two Quince & Ricotta Crumble Squares (page 35), or two batches of Quince & Frangipane Cakes (page 128), with a little left over to top your morning porridge. By all means make a half-quantity if you don't want leftovers, but truly, you will!

Baked Quince

MAKES APPROXIMATELY 500 G (1 LB 2 OZ) BAKED QUINCE

4 quinces (approximately 1.2 kg/
    2 lb 12 oz)
250 ml (9 fl oz) orange juice, plus
    3 long strips of zest
110 g (3¾ oz) caster (superfine)
    sugar
1 cinnamon stick
2 star anise
1 vanilla bean, split and seeds
    scraped (or 1 tablespoon
    vanilla bean paste)

Preheat the oven to 150°C (300°F) fan-forced.

Carefully peel and core the quinces and cut them into eighths. Place the quince slices, orange juice and zest, sugar, cinnamon, star anise and vanilla bean and seeds (or paste) into a large baking dish and toss to combine. Arrange the quince slices in a single layer and cover the dish tightly with foil.

Bake in the preheated oven for 2½–3 hours or until the fruit is beautifully fragrant, tender and ruby-hued. I like to turn the quince slices once during the cooking time and to check that there is still enough liquid in the dish – add a little more orange juice or a splash of water to the tray if it's looking a bit dry.

STORE & SHARE *Allow the fruit to cool, covered, in the tray before using or storing in an airtight container in the fridge for up to 4 days.*

(Pictured on page 215)

Good homemade fruit mince has the remarkable ability to convert even the most die-hard mince pie haters (I know, I used to be one!). I love mine stuffed with prunes and sour cherries, with a good slosh of Pedro Ximénez thrown in for added cheer. Feel free to change the variety of dried fruit to suit your tastes (and what you have in the pantry), just make sure to keep the total weight of fruit to 500 g (1 lb 2 oz). And use the best-quality fruit you can find – it really does make all the difference!

Good Fruit Mince

MAKES APPROXIMATELY 900 G (2 LB) (ENOUGH FOR 2 BATCHES OF MINCE PIES)

200 g (7 oz) pitted prunes,
   roughly chopped
120 g (4¼ oz) dried sour cherries
80 g (2¾ oz) currants
100 g (3½ oz) dried apricots,
   roughly chopped
2 tablespoons Roast Apricot
   Jam (page 206), or marmalade
80 g (2¾ oz) light brown sugar
1 small apple, peeled and grated
1 teaspoon ground cinnamon
1 teaspoon mixed spice
2 teaspoons vanilla bean paste
40 g (1½ oz) unsalted butter
200 ml (7 fl oz) Pedro Ximénez

Combine all the ingredients in a large saucepan. Place over medium-low heat and cook, stirring often, until the butter has melted, the sugar has dissolved and the mixture is bubbling.

STORE & SHARE *Transfer to a sterilised jar (see page 9) or container, allow to cool, then store in the fridge for at least 24 hours, or up to a month, before using.*

(Pictured on page 215)

Thank you

To write a book was a long-held dream of mine. To be asked to write a second is an incredible honour. I count myself exceptionally lucky. There are many people to thank; wonderful folk without whom this book would not have come to be.

To my brilliant publisher, Jane, I thank you. I thank you for your careful guidance, your expert refinement and your unwavering belief in me (especially when my own self-belief had left the building!). It has been a total joy and immense privilege to work with you again.

To Kristy Allen, Virginia Birch, Natalie Crouch and the team at Murdoch Books; oh my goodness, you've done it again! Not only has it been a real delight to work with you a second time, but you have produced a book that once again has exceeded my wildest imaginings. Forever grateful. Kristy, thank you for your careful, calm design-eye. You have impeccable taste, and I love working with you. Virginia, it has been a delight to work with you this year; thank you for making sure everything ran smoothly. I definitely owe you some cake! To Sharon Misko, thank you for your beautiful, considered design.

To my editor, Ariana; thank you for your patience and for once again wrangling my words with such grace and care. It was a pleasure, and one which I hope we get to repeat. To Ines Brenneman, whose beautiful painted backgrounds I have used throughout, your work is magic. I wish you could paint my house!

To my husband, Slav, I said it last time, and I'll say it again; this book could not have happened without your unwavering support, love and restorative cups of tea (so many cups of tea!). Thank you for picking up the slack at home when my head was once again full of cake (and biscuits, buns, slices and tarts this time ...), for always being happy to try one more slice, and for never raising an eyebrow when I said I need to test a recipe just One. More. Time. I love you.

To my dear Olive and Kip; my best creations, never to be eclipsed. I love you. And I'm sorry for trying to pass off sweet bakes as dinner sometimes. Next year we'll eat more salad.

To my mum and dad; at the risk of repeating myself, thank you for everything, always. Mum, thank you once again for reading every word before anyone else did and for correcting my grammar with such aplomb. Thank you for carefully testing many of the recipes in this book, and for blaming your oven, not my recipes, if they ever didn't quite work out as planned! Dad, thank you for letting me raid your vegetable and fruit garden. Your rhubarb is truly excellent.

To my friends and neighbours who diligently worked their way through box after box of baked goods. Thank you! And please know that if I gifted you cake, you are very dear to me – I could only cope with feedback from people I truly love during the testing process ...

And finally, thank you to all of you who have inspired and supported me over the years. To those of you who took *The Plain Cake Appreciation Society* into your hearts and homes, I cannot thank you enough. I feel honoured and humbled by your support and companionship. I hope you can find room in your kitchens for one more book. x

Index

Published in 2025 by Murdoch Books, an imprint of Allen & Unwin

Murdoch Books Australia
Cammeraygal Country
83 Alexander Street
Crows Nest NSW 2065
Phone: +61 (0)2 8425 0100
murdochbooks.com.au
info@murdochbooks.com.au

Murdoch Books UK
Ormond House
26–27 Boswell Street
London WC1N 3JZ
Phone: +44 (0) 20 8785 5995
murdochbooks.co.uk
info@murdochbooks.co.uk

For corporate orders and custom publishing,
contact our business development team
at salesenquiries@murdochbooks.com.au

Publisher: Jane Morrow
Editorial Manager: Virginia Birch
Design Manager: Kristy Allen
Designer: Sharon Misko
Editor: Ariana Klepac
Photography, recipes and styling: Tilly Pamment
Production Manager: Natalie Crouch

*Murdoch Books acknowledges the Traditional Owners
of the Country on which we live and work. We pay our
respects to all Aboriginal and Torres Strait Islander
Elders, past and present.*

ISBN 978 1 76150 031 2

A catalogue record for this
book is available from the
National Library of Australia

A catalogue record for this book is
available from the British Library

Colour reproduction by Splitting Image
Colour Studio Pty Ltd, Wantirna, Victoria
Printed in China by C&C Offset Printing Co., Ltd.

OVEN GUIDE: You may find cooking times
vary depending on the oven you are using.
For conventional ovens, as a general rule, set
the oven temperature to 20°C (25–50°F) hotter
than indicated in the recipe.

TABLESPOON MEASURES: We have used 20 ml
(4 teaspoon) tablespoon measures. If you are using a
15 ml (3 teaspoon) tablespoon, add an extra teaspoon
of the ingredient for each tablespoon specified.

IMPORTANT: Those who might be at risk from
the effects of salmonella poisoning (the elderly,
pregnant women, young children and those suffering
from immune deficiency diseases) should consult
their doctor with any concerns about eating raw eggs.

For recipes labelled 'gluten free', the ingredients
included are typically gluten free, however it is the
reader's responsibility to check that specific brands of
the product you are using (icing/confectioner's sugar,
baking powder, etc.) do not contain gluten. The author
and/or publisher cannot be held responsible for any
adverse reactions.

10 9 8 7 6 5 4 3 2 1

MIX
Paper | Supporting
responsible forestry
FSC® C008047

About the Author

Tilly Pamment is an Australian recipe writer, photographer and stylist. She lives in the Blue Mountains in New South Wales with her husband and two children and here – in between chasing kids around – she photographs food and flowers, and writes seasonal baking recipes.

Tilly writes a monthly baking column for *Country Style*, and her love of good, simple cake was celebrated in her first book, *The Plain Cake Appreciation Society*.

Tilly is the creative brain behind @tillys_table, where she shares recipes and inspiration with a community of like-minded pleasure seekers.